A Constellation
for Quilters

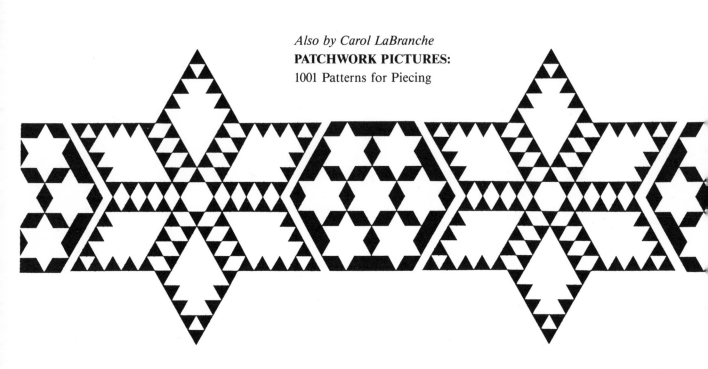

Also by Carol LaBranche
PATCHWORK PICTURES:
1001 Patterns for Piecing

A Constellation for Quilters

STAR PATTERNS FOR PIECING

by Carol LaBranche

Patterns rendered by
John Fox, Frank Mahood, and Lisa Magaz

THE MAIN STREET PRESS • PITTSTOWN, NEW JERSEY

This book is dedicated to Peter Mayer. The dear memory of my new ("step" is too harsh a prefix) father keeps me as warm and comforted as the most beautiful quilt ever made.

First edition 1986

All rights reserved

Copyright © 1986 by Carol LaBranche

Published by
The Main Street Press, Inc.
William Case House
Pittstown, NJ 08867

Published simultaneously in Canada by
Methuen Publications
2330 Midland Ave.
Agincourt, Ontario M1S 1P7

Printed in the United States of America

Text and cover/jacket design by Frank Mahood

10 9 8 7 6 5 4 3 2 1

Library of Congress Cataloging in Publication Data

Contents

Preface

MY first quilt book, *Patchwork Pictures,* left me with a guilty conscience. It contained over a thousand representational pieced patterns (birds, baskets, hearts) but did not include any patterns for stars. There was a good reason, of course. Quilt authorities like Phyllis Haders and Carrie Hall said that the star patterns outnumbered all other kinds of designs. They ventured that there were probably over a hundred of them . . . too many for my book already bulging with airplanes, rose gardens, and butterflies. So, I carefully refrained from mentioning how nice stars looked over houses, boats, and trees, but vowed to buy a telescope and start searching the quilt heavens for stars.

They weren't hard to find. What was hard was deciding what was a star and what wasn't. Sunflowers, sunbursts, snowflakes, and mariner's compasses all have points; couldn't they be stars too? Quilt names were no help. Some obvious stars are called something else entirely, while some patterns with "star" in the traditional name resemble anything but. And, of course, there is the well known Quilt Name Muddle, with the same name being used for different patterns and the same patterns having different names. I quickly gave up letting names be my guide and settled on common sense and my good pair of eyes. If the pattern looked like a star, I included it. If it didn't, I didn't. Subjective, I know, so I hastily accede to any complaints. If you find a pattern here that you think is not a star, I agree. If I've left out your favorite star, I'm sorry.

Having given myself the cosmic power of deciding what was a star, the next problem was finding a suitable way to organize the sheer abundance of them. Again, the traditional names were of absolutely no use. After I had a folder full of Lemon, Variable, and Sawtooth Stars there were still many more stars whose names matched nothing at all. Next, I tried to group together the stars that looked alike. My common sense and good pair of eyes were not equal to the task. I got starry eyed, literally, trying to find similarities in the over 600 different patterns I'd collected. Finally, in one of those great AH HA moments, I woke up in the middle of the night with the simple solution. Count the number of points. So the stars are listed according to how many points they have, beginning with four and ending with more than eight. Two additional chapters have Feathered Stars (so flamboyant they insisted on remaining separate), Stars and Stripes (just for fun), and Shooting Stars (this is the year of Halley's Comet). Points are counted at the outermost edge of the star, as some stars have a different number of secondary "points" inside the design. Curiously, there are no seven-pointed stars, or at least none that I could find. Some mystery of mathematics perhaps? If you have a pieced seven-pointed star pattern, I'd love to see it; send it on to the publisher. Appliqué doesn't count, though; all the patterns in this book are for piecing.

So, here are the stars to make a heavenly quilt. And goodbye guilty conscience!

Introduction: How To Use These Patterns

THIS book contains over 600 star patterns for the quilter. Some are very simple and appropriate for the beginner, others need a more experienced hand. But easy or less so, a basic understanding of quilt mechanics is necessary. Fortunately, the novice quilter has many places to go for help. Fabric and quilt stores offer year-around classes, friends are often good teachers, and several excellent books are available to guide the beginner through the whole process of making a quilt. The books in the bibliography by Beth Gutcheon, Carla Hassel and Kaye Wood are especially recommended in this regard. Other writers have specifically addressed the piecing of stars, notably the Lone Star and Feathered Star, and their books may be useful to even the knowledgeable quilter in avoiding problems and working more efficiently. These books, by Jean Dubois, Marsha McCloskey, and Blanche and Helen Young, are also in the bibliography.

DESIGN

STARS are versatile. In one quilt they can be big or small, varied or similiar, scattered or lined up like soldiers. Briefly, here are some of the many possibilities.

1. *One large star.* The star quilt that shines in my memory is an Amish Sawtooth. It had one big black star on a field of deep, glowing orange. Simplicity itself, the quilt had only a few long sewing lines and a startling color choice. I've never forgotten it.

2. *Stars within stars.* This has a long and honorable tradition and is fun to boot. Every chapter has at least a few of these Chinese boxes, with the one in the Feathered Star chapter a real whopper. With some graph paper, some fiddling, and a little imagination, a quilter can construct any number of stars within stars, just by fitting one inside another. Keep the kinds of stars simple, though, or the point(s) will be lost.

3. *Use stars not as pure pointy pattern, but for their meaning.* They naturally belong with Delectable Mountains, Log Cabins, and Pine Trees. And don't forget them when making a Christmas quilt. Or do a Milky Way with an indigo background or a study guide to beginning astronomy.

4. *Try a sample quilt using all stars.* If you want an extra challenge, design one without the traditional straight up and down sashing.

5. *Stars are born to use up scraps.* Be silly and do flowered stars or serious and sew geometric or striped stars.

6. *Look for secondary star patterns in the corners of the block.* Most of the shooting stars have them, and they can be found in all of the other chapters, too. With some color planning you can get an extra star out of every four blocks. What a bargain!

7. *Stars are made for color reversals.* Try dark ones on light, bright stars on dark, or use up that silver lamé or neon Dayglo that has been seen lurking in your fabric collection.

8. *Most stars look well with most other stars,* with the few exceptions noted in the individual chapter introductions. Pick all of one kind of star (four-pointed, Sawtooth, etc.) and make all the variations.

9. *Stars come in many different sizes.* Try making a quilt in which each block is not the same size. It will take a bit more figuring when it comes to combining the blocks, but, again, the inherent compatibility of one star with another will help in the final design.

10. *Don't forget to add a star border.*

CONVERTING THE STAR PATTERNS TO QUILT BLOCKS

THE ancient Egyptians used the grid method to enlarge their designs from books of patterns much like this one. By placing a grid over a painted model in a book, and then a larger scale grid on a wall, they could accurately reproduce any design or image to any size without skill in drafting. The same neat trick works just as well for modern quilters. The only stars that defy the precise grid method are the String stars. The piecing of these is irregular. Do with them what you will. There are only a few and these are clearly indicated.

The quilter must only determine what size block(s) are needed for the quilt. Round numbers, easily divisible, are the best size for any block. Six, 8, or 12-inch blocks are easier than 5, 7, or 11-inch blocks.

Next draw the block full size on graph paper. If the pattern in this book is 4 squares wide and 4 squares high, and an 8-inch block is needed, then each square on your graph paper will be 2 inches. Two x 4 = 8. This is the most difficult math needed. Graph paper doesn't come with 2-inch squares, of course, but it is easy enough to rule off 2 inches on any scale graph paper. They all use the inch as the standard length of measurement. Many graph papers have a heavier rule at each inch, to make this point clear.

Now, using quilter's common sense, determine the easiest way to piece the star, using the fewest number of pattern pieces. For instance, the Sawtooth Star is easy. There are three pieces needed—two squares (1 and 3) and a triangle (2). It is much

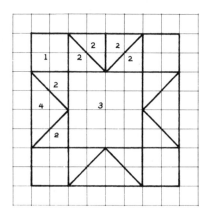

harder to piece the star if four pieces are used, even though the triangle (4) is bigger than the two small triangles (2) that make it up. It is easier to sew the two small triangles together than to try to fit the larger triangle in-between the two smaller ones. Look for ease of construction and the fewest number of pieces, not necessarily the biggest possible pieces.

All star patterns are symmetrical, which makes analyzing them simpler. Even the big Feathered Stars are made up of easily identifiable units which repeat themselves. When faced with a forbiddingly complicated star, don't despair. Take one of two approaches: either quarter the design, and do only one quarter; the other three quarters will be identical. Or, do one point and look again; all the points are the same. As an example, study this Feathered Star.

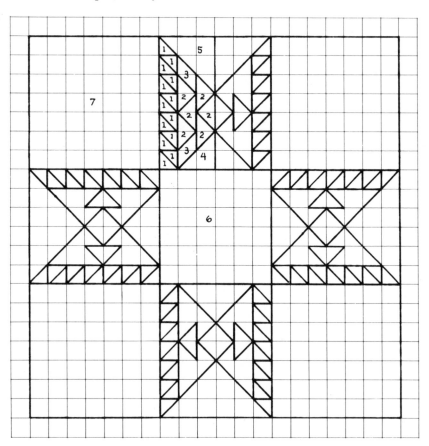

Sew all the 1's together to make the feathers, then the 2's together to make two sets of truncated pyramids. Add the 3's to the ends of one set. Sew the feathers to the first set of pyramids (the ones with the 3's), and then that combined pieced to the second set of pyramids. Add triangles 4 and 5 to each side and one point is finished. Note that there are only five pattern pieces. The other seven points are identical; just repeat the process. Big squares 6 and 7 complete the star. Analyzing stars is a neat game, with the object being ease of sewing and the fewest pattern pieces. Once played successfully, it's a lot more fun than Monopoly and you always pass GO.

Finally, make templates the exact size of each pattern piece. It is not considered cheating to use ready-made templates made of metal or plastic. They will be more durable than paper templates, and you can be confident of their accuracy. Nineteenth-century quilters happily bought tin patterns from the traveling peddler. Modern quilters need only journey to the nearest quilt store. If your pattern pieces can't be found in the standard-size sets of templates, or you just want to do it yourself, I recommend Beth Gutcheon's and Judy Martin's books (see bibliography). Both give directions for making templates for both hand and machine sewing, regular or windowpane ones.

Templates in hand, start cutting, and Merry Quilt Making!

A Constellation for Quilters

1. Four-Pointed Stars

FOUR-POINTED STARS have lots of possibilities, even though they have the minimum number of points a star can have. There are seventy-nine different stars in this chapter and most of them can be varied considerably through color choice. The same star will look completely different, depending on whether it is pieced in two, three, or four colors.

The four-pointed stars are divided into four categories. First come those whose points go in the four cardinal directions. Then come the stars whose points are in the corners of the block. Next are the odd cousins, the pinwheel stars, that insist on going their own offbeat way. Finally there are irregular designs. For design purposes it is usually better not to mix the four kinds of stars. All of the stars in each of the first three categories will look comfortable together, but often will not combine well with those in the other two groups. The irregulars only stand by themselves.

15

Cardinal Points

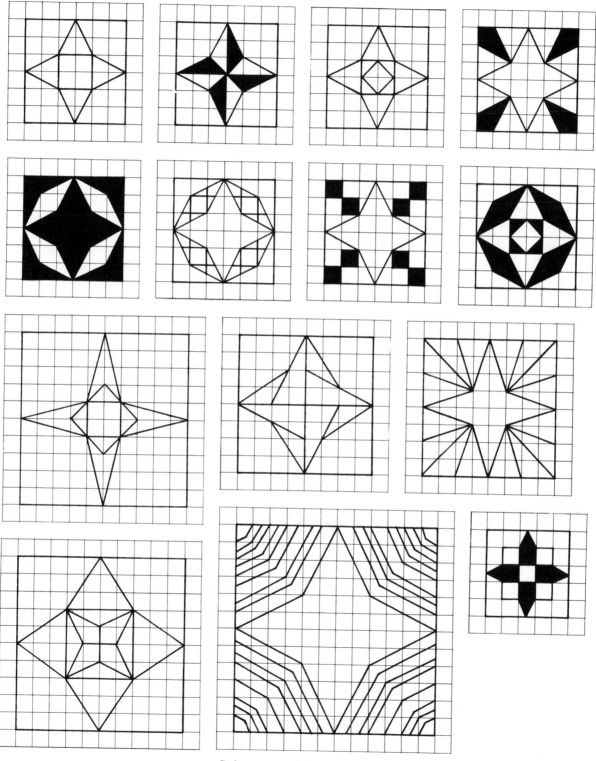

String star requiring irregular piecing.

Cardinal Points, Continued

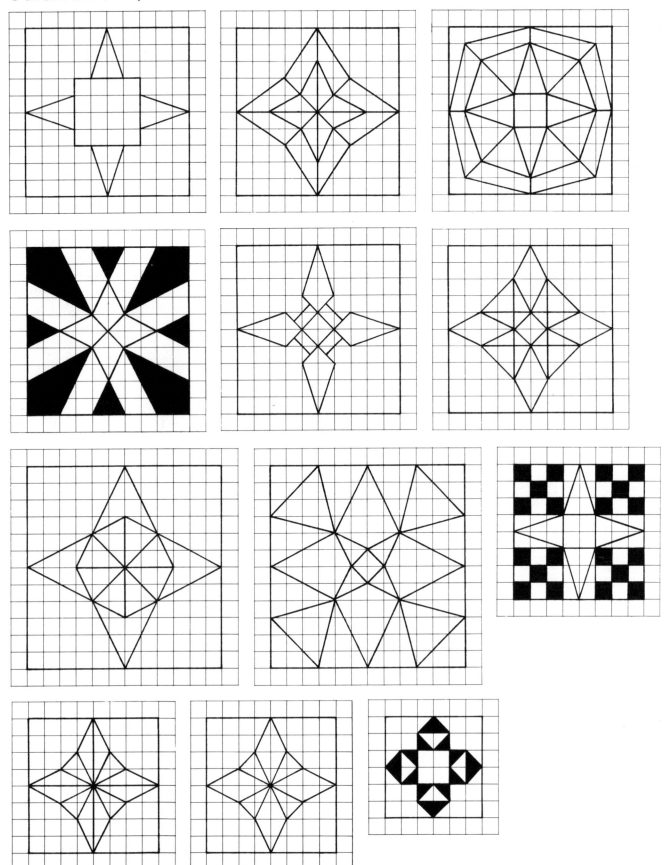

Cardinal Points, Continued

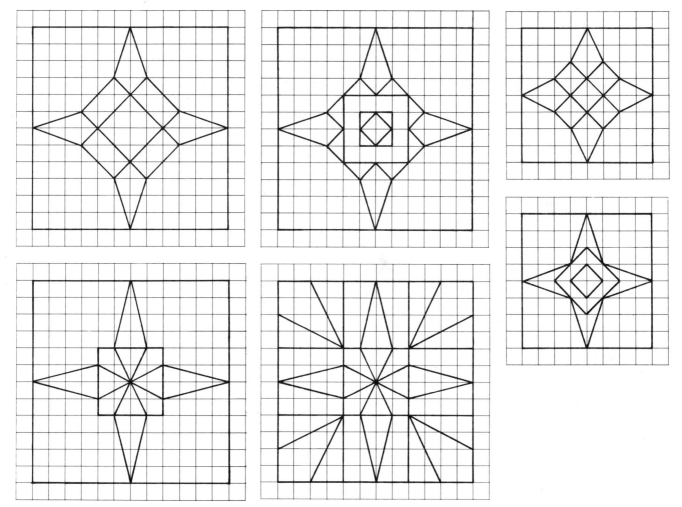

Points in Corners

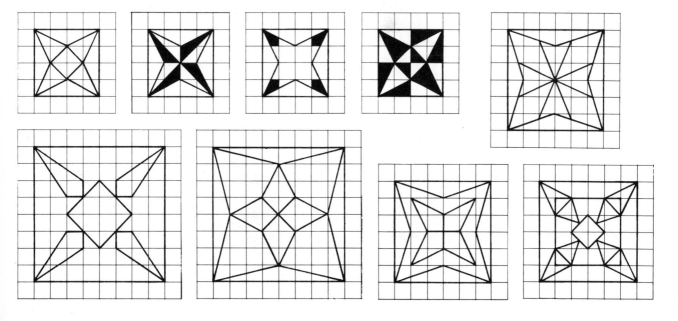

Points in Corners, Continued

String star requiring irregular piecing.

Pinwheel

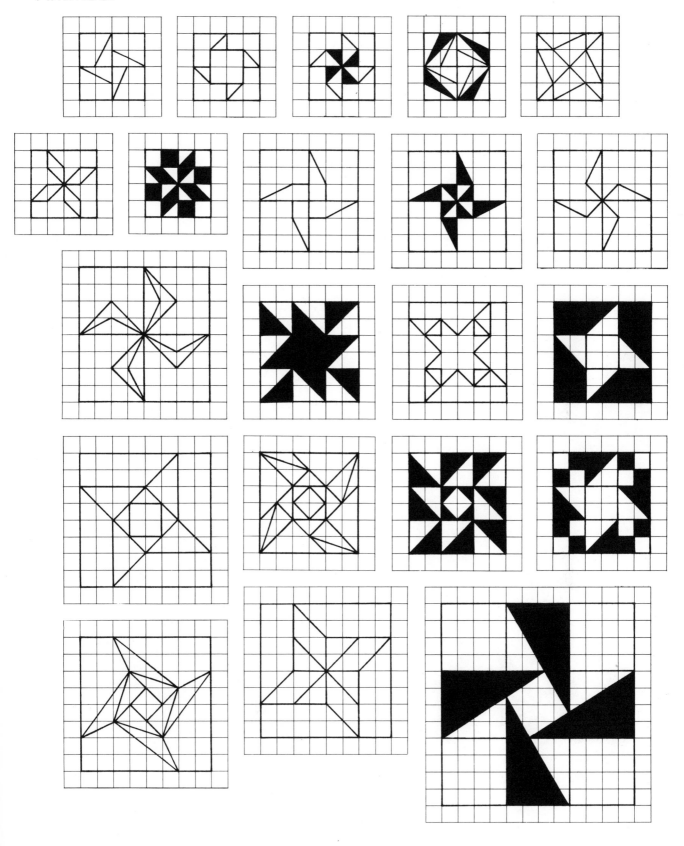

Irregular

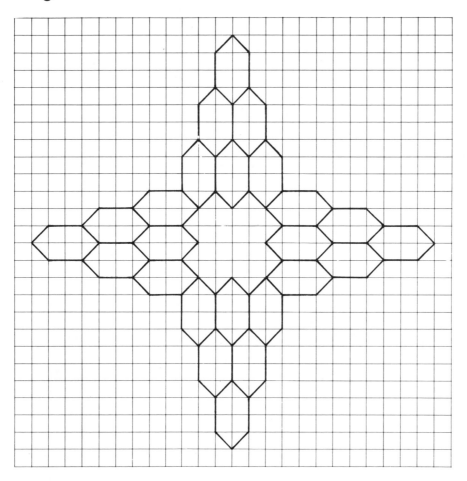

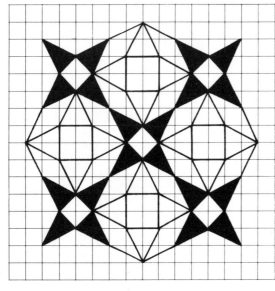

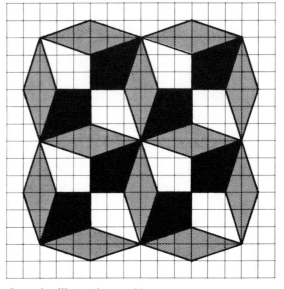

See color illustration, p. 33.

2. Five-Pointed Stars

STARS are most commonly drawn with five points, but five-pointed stars are rare in the quilt sky. They appeared briefly for the Bicentennial, but quickly disappeared. They aren't even common in Texas, where the name Texas Star always means a five-pointer. This lack of popularity probably comes from the difficulty of drafting one from scratch. It can be done by the traditional paper-folding method, but it takes an origami wizard to do it. A better alternative is offered in the following pages. Happily, once drafted, a five-pointed star is relatively easy to piece. The simplest star needs only five pattern pieces. Since the hard work of drafting is done in this book, hopefully there will soon be more five-pointed stars in the sky.

Step 1

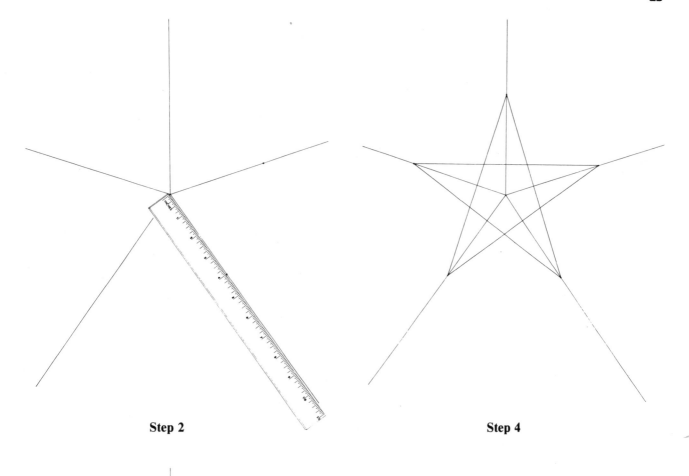

Step 2

Step 4

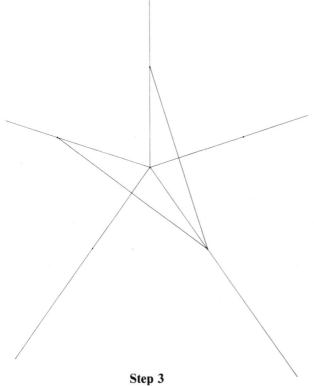

Step 3

STEPS FOR DRAFTING A FIVE-POINTED STAR

1. Very carefully trace the five radiating spokes from this page. If you choose to use a copy machine rather than tracing, be sure the machine does not produce a distorted image.

2. With a ruler, carefully mark off the same distance from the center on all five spokes. This distance should be a little more than half the width of the star you wish to create.

3. After marking off the equal distances, begin by connecting every other point.

4. Proceed around the whole axis until every dot is connected.

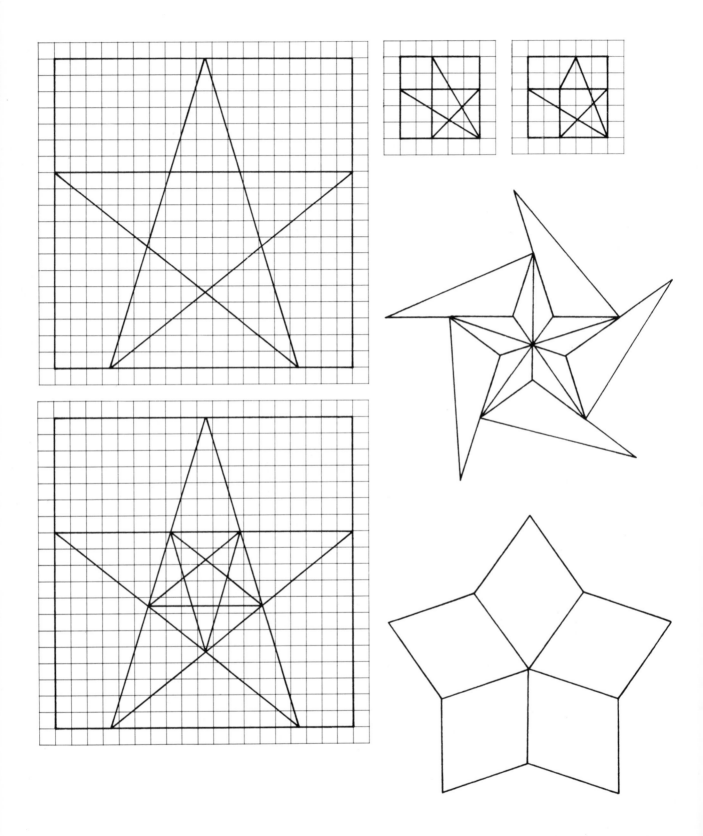

3. Six-Pointed Stars

SIX-POINTED STARS are fat little stars with a lot of twinkle power. Most, with very few exceptions, are based on the hexagon form. In this chapter they are divided into two groups: those whose points fit into the corners of the hexagon block and those whose points touch the sides of the hexagon. The two types of stars join easily, but their points will seem to stab each other if the stars are used too close together. Make good design use of this effect, or plan to use stars from only one group. Fortunately, there are enough interesting and challenging stars in each category to create a full blue-sky quilt without any trouble. Also included in this chapter are eleven designs which are not worked within the basic hexagon form.

A set of instructions is provided in the following pages for drafting the basic hexagon form and either of the two types of stars. In addition, there are instructions for drafting a six-pointed star made of a circle of equal-sized squares.

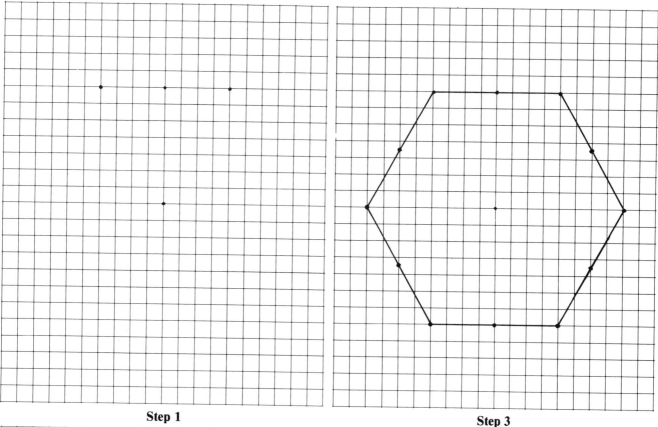

Step 1

Step 3

Step 2

DRAFTING A HEXAGON AND A SIX-POINTED STAR ON A SQUARE GRID

1. Mark the center point of the grid; count up seven spaces (squares) and mark point. Finally, count off four spaces to the left and right of the top point and mark these side points.

2. Count off eight spaces on both sides of the center point and mark off these side points. Repeat step 1, counting down seven spaces, and then over four spaces left and right. Mark these points.

3. Rule a connecting line between all the outer points to produce a hexagon. Find the center of each of the four angled sides by marking the intersection of the angled and the vertical grid lines two spaces in from the outer left and right points. Mark the centers of the angled sides.

Step 4

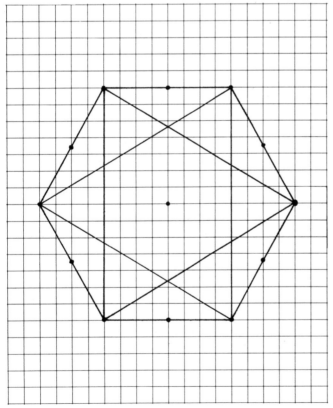

Step 5

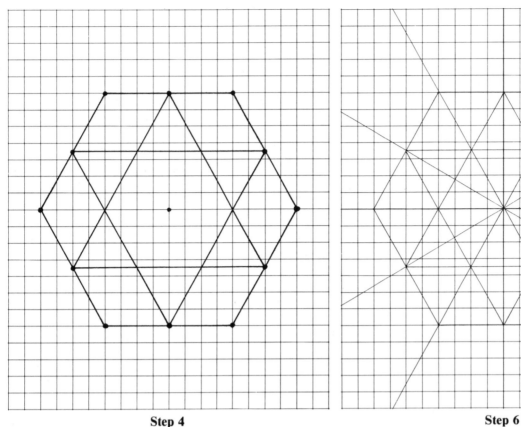

Step 6

4. By connecting every other center of the six sides, you will create a six-pointed star within the hexagon, a star whose points touch the sides of the hexagon.

5. For a star whose points fit into the corners of the hexagon block, connect every other corner point.

6. By drawing straight lines through opposite corner points and opposite center side points, you will produce twelve equidistant radiating lines from the center. These will facilitate the drawing of hexagons of different scales that do not coincide with grid lines (see p. 134, Feathered Stars).

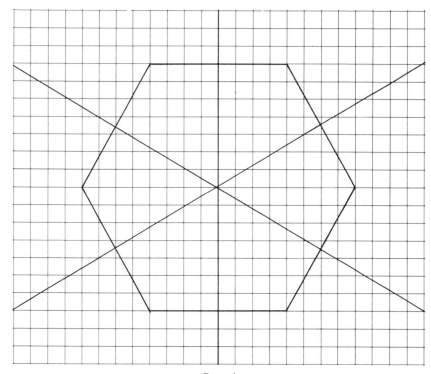

Step 1

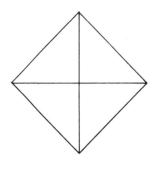

Step 3

INSTRUCTIONS FOR DRAFTING A SIX-POINTED STAR MADE OF A CIRCLE OF EQUAL-SIZED SQUARES.

1. Draw a hexagon and add radiating lines through the center side points as previously described for the star on a square grid.

2. On a side which coincides with the grid lines, draw a square, counting up and down four spaces each. Mark these points and connect them with the corner points at the ends of that side.

3. Make a tracing of this square. Include the inner diagonal lines.

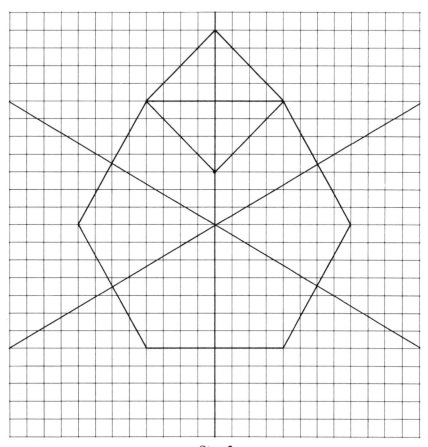

Step 2

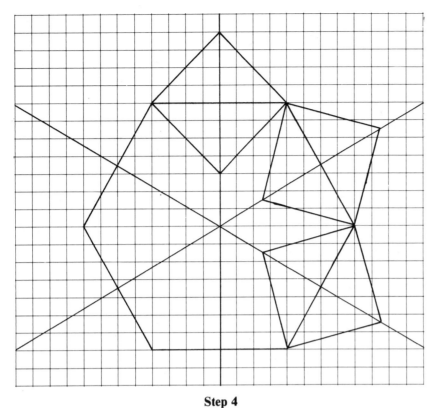

Step 4

4. Complete the star by overlaying this square piece around each of the six sides of the hexagon. The diagonal lines of the square should always coincide with the hexagon side and the radiating line.

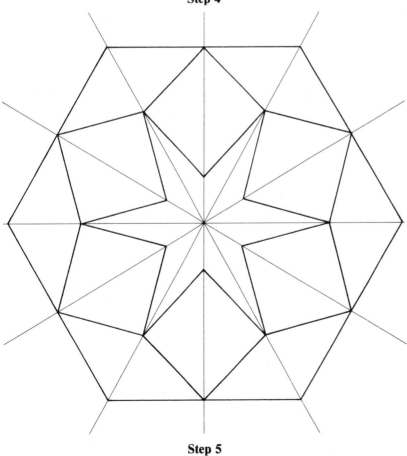

Step 5

5. Completed star pattern.

Points Touching Sides

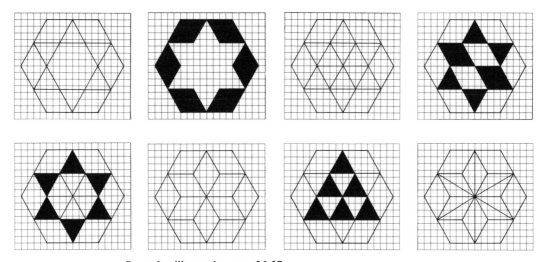

See color illustration, pp. 36-37.

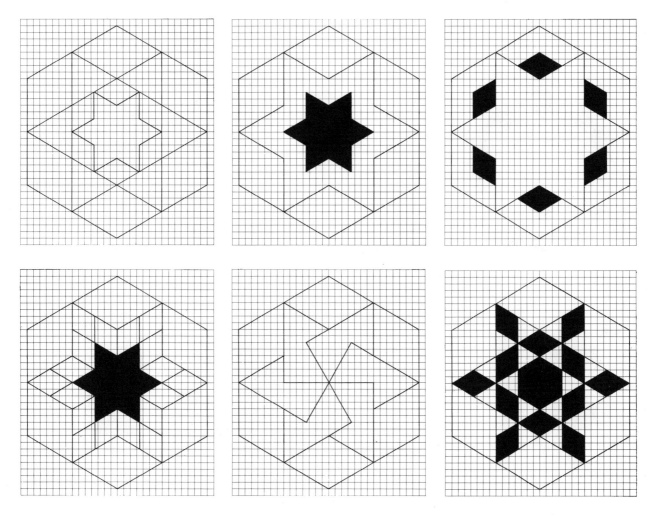

Points Touching Sides, Continued

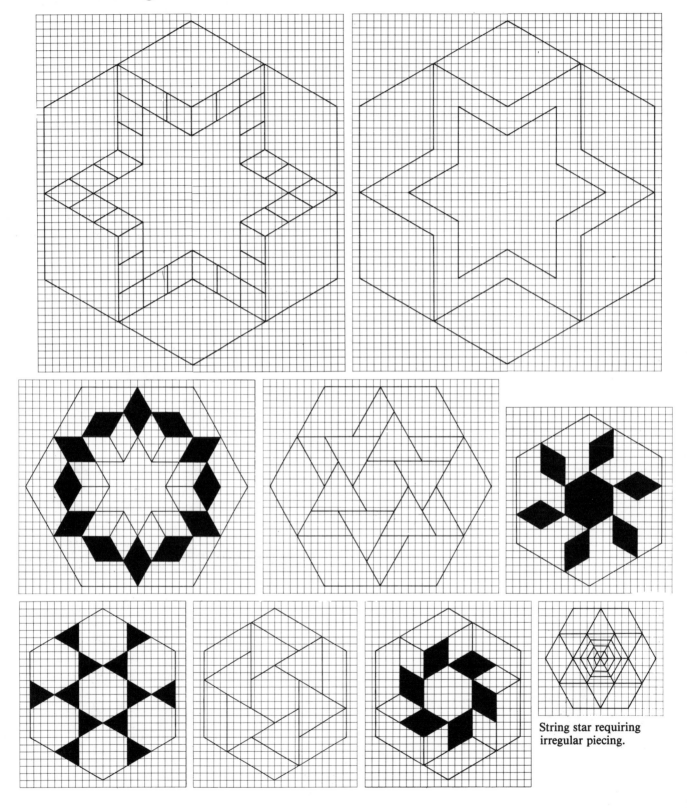

String star requiring
irregular piecing.

"Arkansas Snowflake," Ohio, c. 1870-80, pieced wool challis, 75" x 88". See black-and-white design on p. 20. Laura Fisher Antique Quilts and Americana.

34

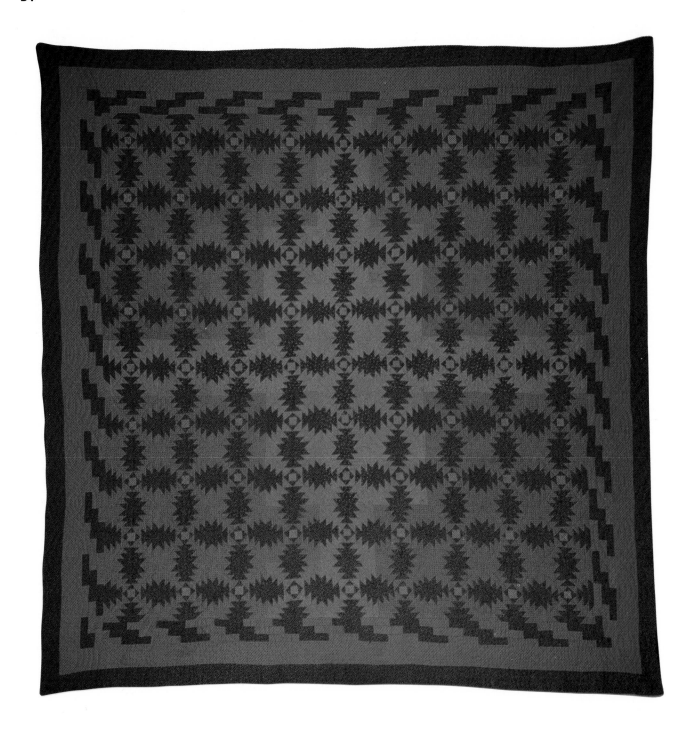

"Pineapple," Pennsylvania, c. 1880-90, pieced cotton, 80″ square. See black-and-white design of a Feathered four-pointed star on p. 120. Collection of The Pink House, New Hope, Pennsylvania.

"Columbia Star," Midwest, c. 1930, pieced cotton, 80″ x 90″. See black-and-white design on p. 45.
Laura Fisher Antique Quilts and Americana.

"Tumbling Blocks," Pennsylvania, c. 1880, pieced silk and velvet, 53″ x 67″. See black-and-white design on p. 31. Laura Fisher Antique Quilts and Americana.

"Variable Star," California, c. 1880, pieced cotton, 50″ x 52″. See black-and-white design of an eight-pointed star on p. 75. Collection of Phyllis Haders.

"Nine Stars," Pennsylvania, c. 1880, pieced cotton, 98″ square. See black-and-white design of an eight-pointed LeMoyne or Lemon star on p. 54. Collection of The Pink House, New Hope, Pennsylvania.

"Star of Bethlehem," Ohio, c. 1845, pieced cotton, 83″ square. See black-and-white design on p. 55.
Laura Fisher Antique Quilts and Americana.

Points Touching Sides, Continued

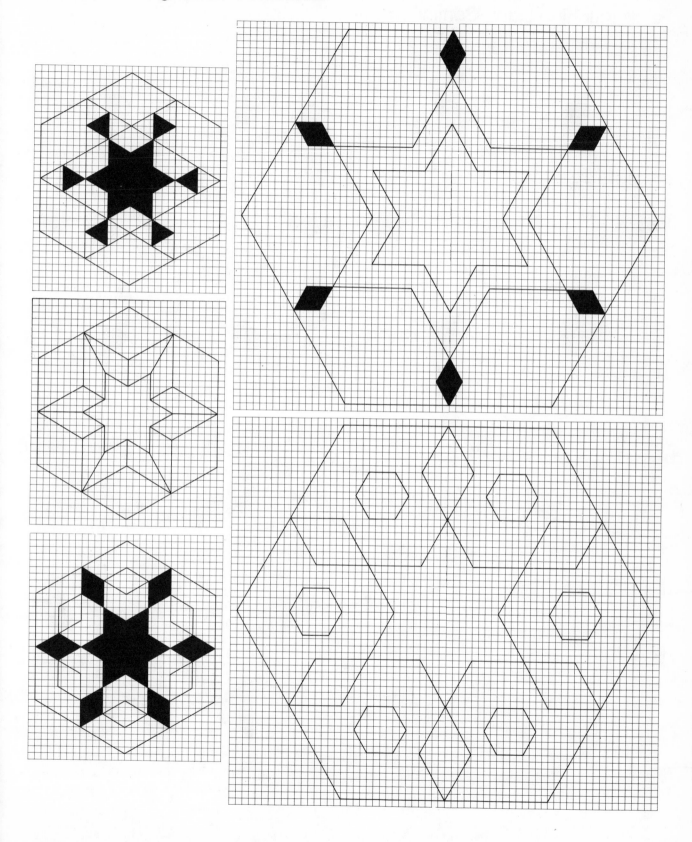

Points Touching Sides, Continued

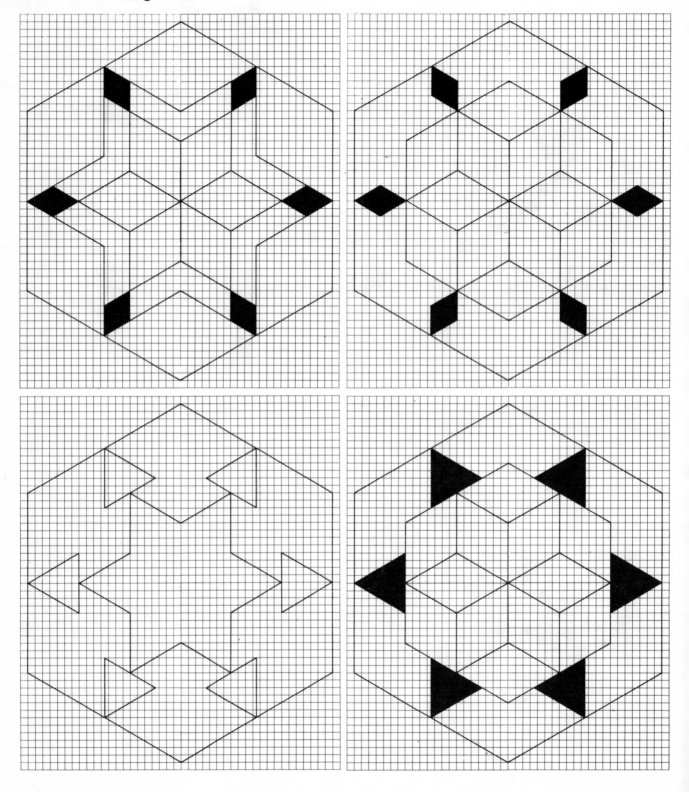

Points Touching Sides, Continued

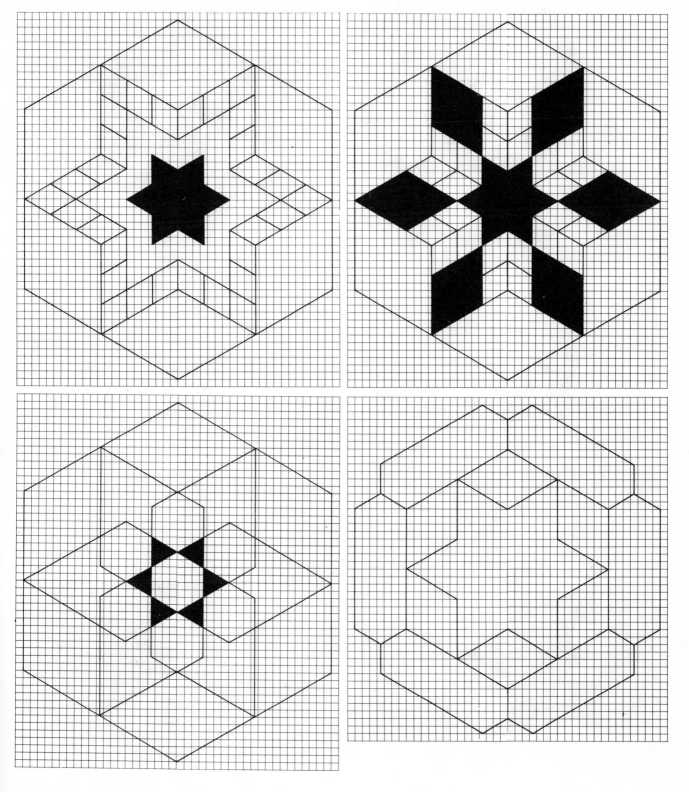

Points Toucning Sides, Continued

Points Touching Sides, Continued

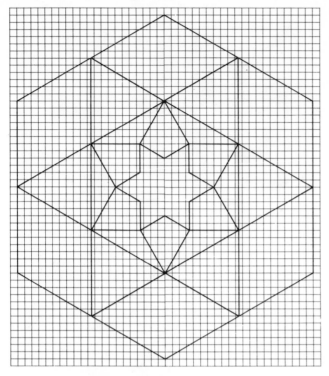
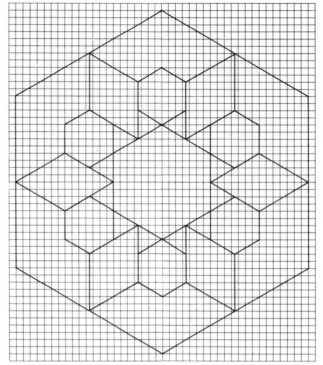

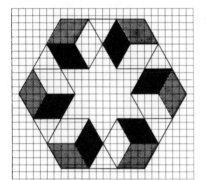
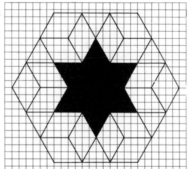
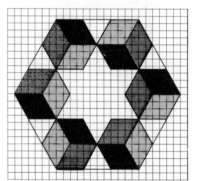

See color illustration, p. 35.

Points in Corners

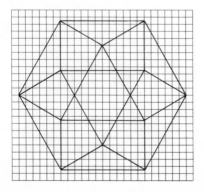
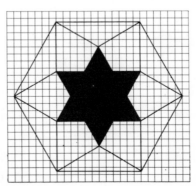
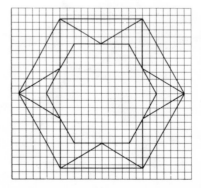

Points in Corners, Continued

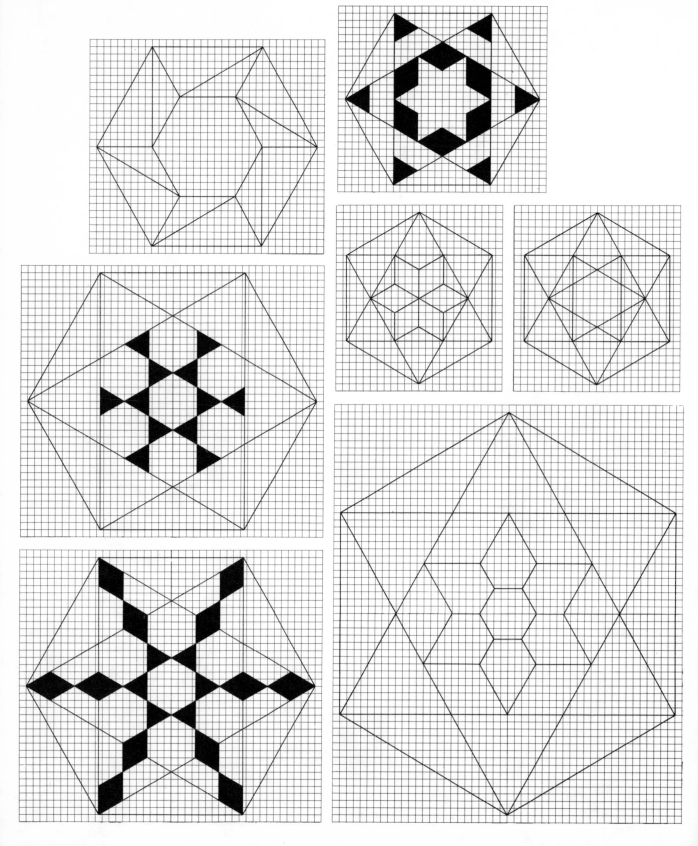

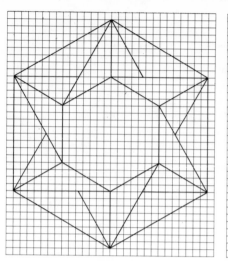
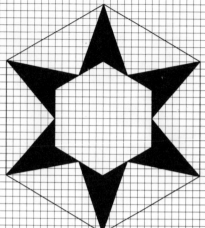
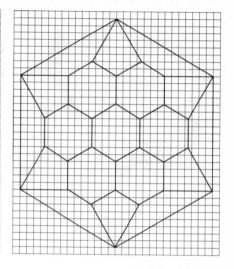

Irregular

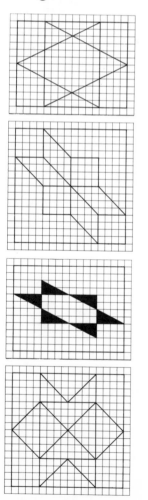

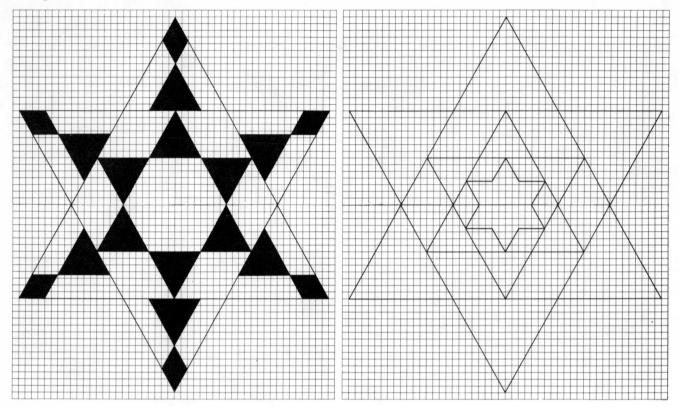

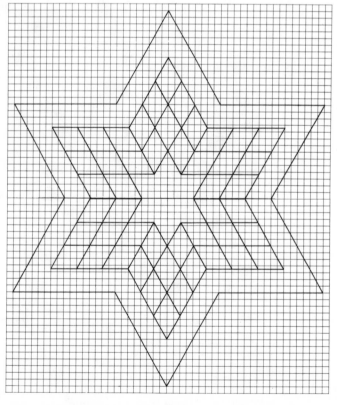

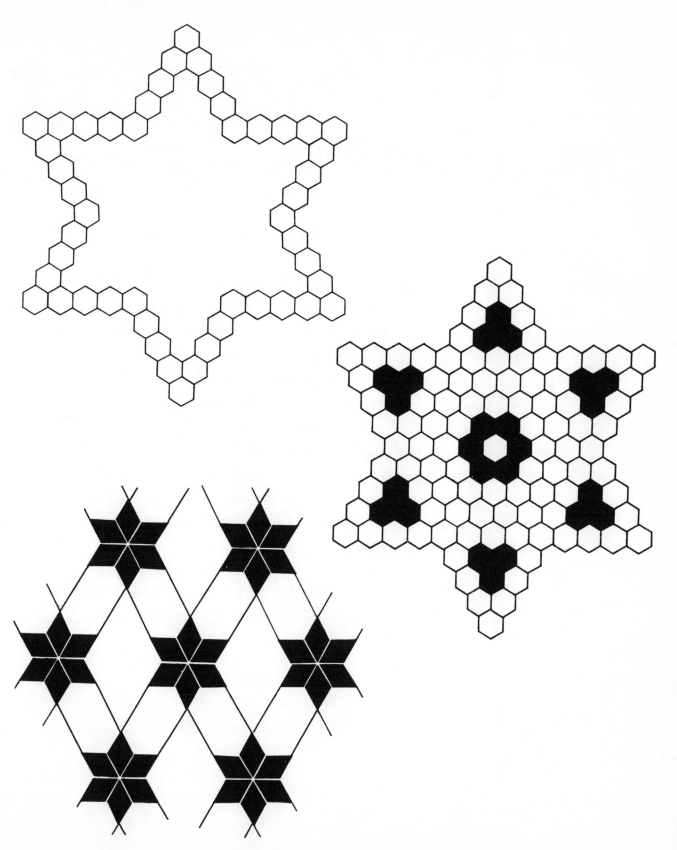

4. Eight-Pointed Stars

THERE are nearly 250 stars in this chapter, including different types of the three best known—Lemon (or LeMoyne), Pieced (or Sawtooth), and Variable (or Ohio). The old favorites, Lone Star, Star of Bethlehem, and Broken Star, are all essentially extensions of the Lemon Star and are included with them. The great variety in Lemon Star quilts is due largely to color choice and not to variations in the basic pattern. The opposite is true of the Pieced Star, of which there are over seventy-five versions and probably more waiting to be found in the outer galaxies. The Ohio or Variable Star varies only in color and proportion, but not in basic pattern which remains fairly stable. After these three stars come all of the unnamed stars of the eight-point cosmos divided into regular and irregular categories. They are arranged in order of relative scale. Stars that fit into a 6 x 6 grid come first, then 7 x 7, then 8 x 8, and so on.

Special instructions for drafting a Lemon Star pattern follow.

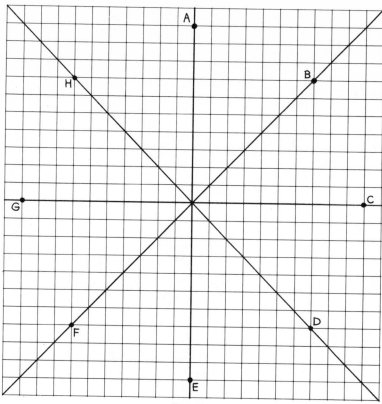

Step 1

DRAFTING A LEMON STAR

1. On graph paper rule in the vertical and horizontal lines intersecting a central point. Then rule in diagonal lines that also meet in the center. Count ten spaces from the center point on the vertical and horizontal lines in both directions and mark the points A, C, E, and G. Finally, count seven spaces from the center point on the diagonal lines in all directions and mark the points B, D, F, and H.

2. Take any point and draw a connecting line to the two points closest to the opposite point (A to D, A to F; B to E, B to G; etc.). Complete these connections for all outer points.

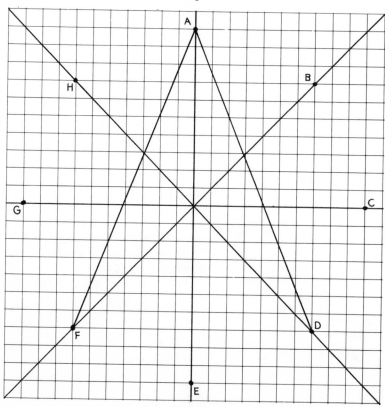

Step 2

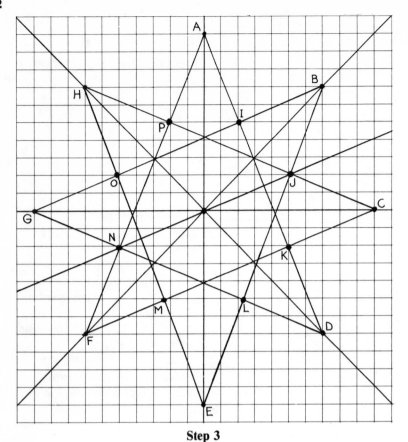

Step 3

3. Mark the spots for the inner points where the lines drawn in step 2 intersect—I, J, K, L, M, N, O, and P. Mark very carefully as the points will not coincide exactly with the grid lines.

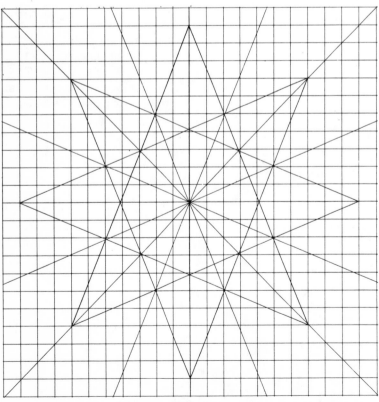

Step 4

4. Connect the center point with its two opposite inner points—N to J, O to K, P to L, etc. You will then have a complete eight-pointed star.

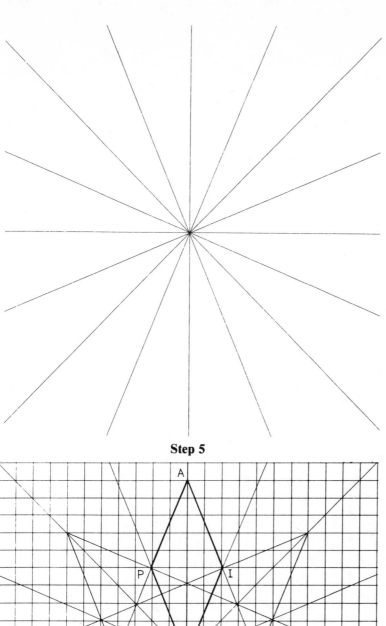

Step 5

Step 6a

5. Trace all of the radiating lines that have been created on tracing paper.

6a and b. Trace a diamond shape on tracing paper. This is the shape produced by connecting the center point and outer point with the two inner points at each side (center to P, P to A, A to I, I to center).

Step 6b

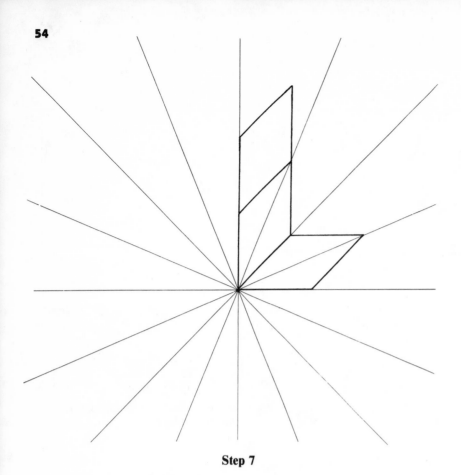

7. Start building the final Lemon Star pattern by tracing repeated diamond shapes in rows along the radiating lines.

Step 7

8. The completed block can take the form shown here. This same design is seen in color on p. 39.

Step 8

Lemon Stars

Star of Bethlehem

See color illustration, p. 89.

Lemon Stars, Continued

Lemon Stars, Continued

Pieced/Sawtooth Stars

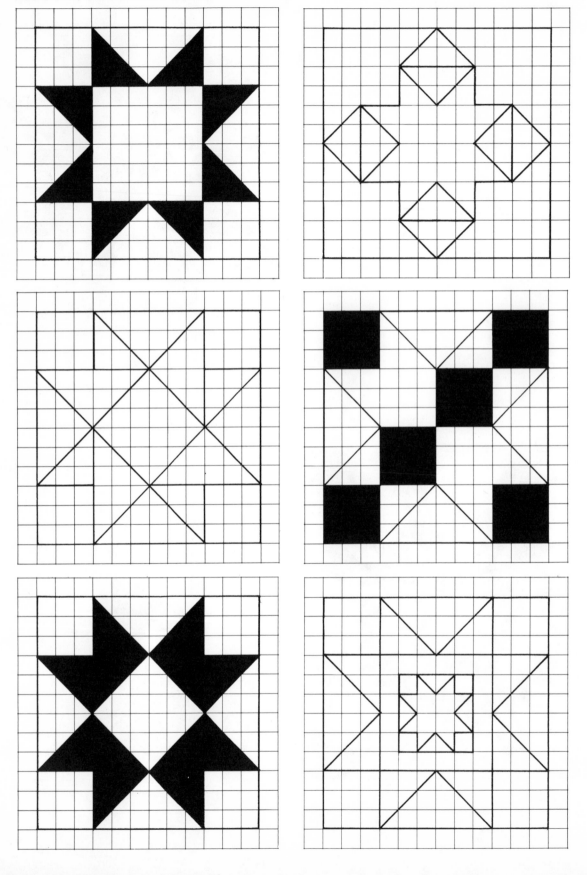

Pieced/Sawtooth Stars, Continued

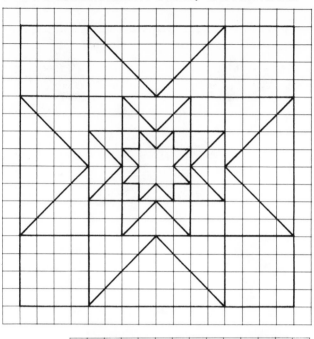

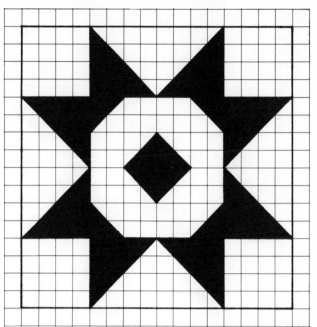

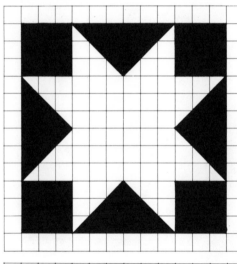

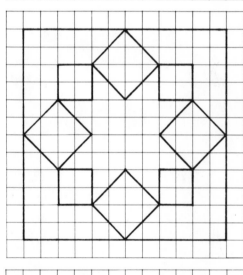

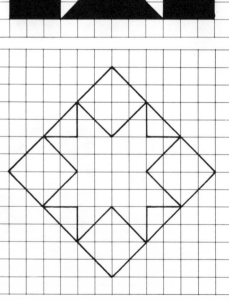

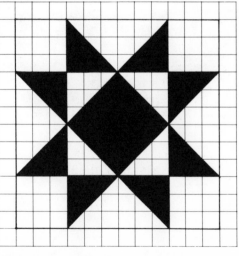

Pieced/Sawtooth Stars, Continued

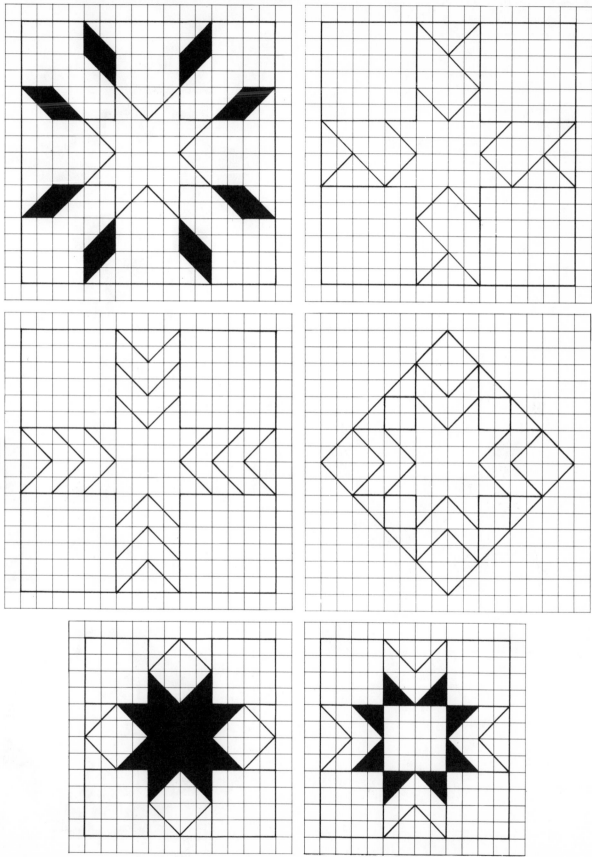

Pieced/Sawtooth Stars, Continued

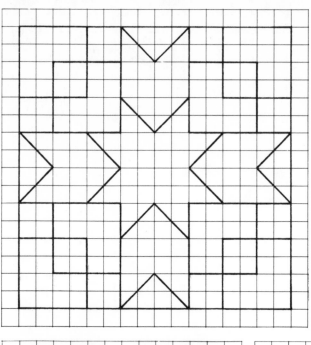

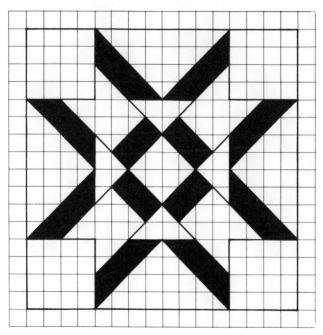

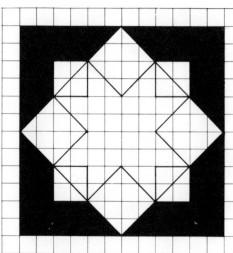

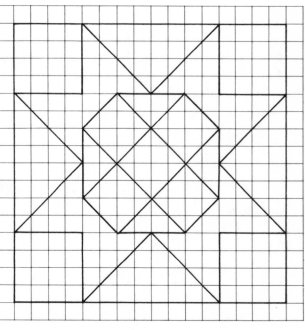

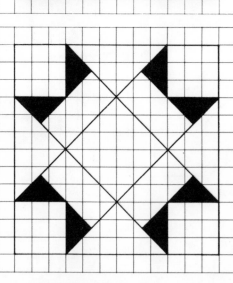

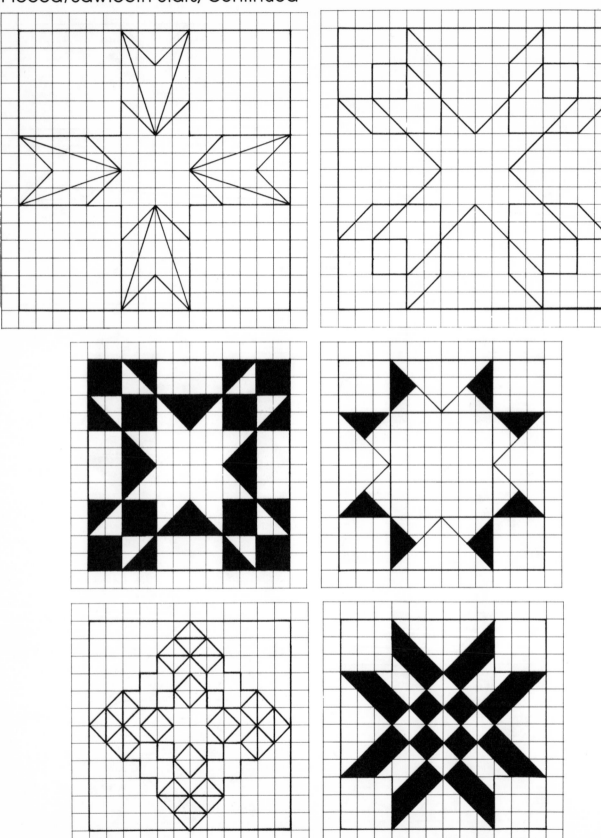

Pieced/Sawtooth Stars, Continued

Pieced/Sawtooth Stars, Continued

Pieced/Sawtooth Stars, Continued

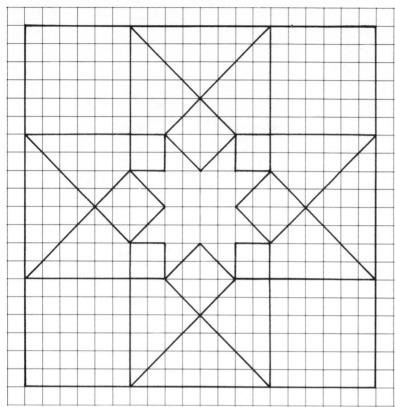

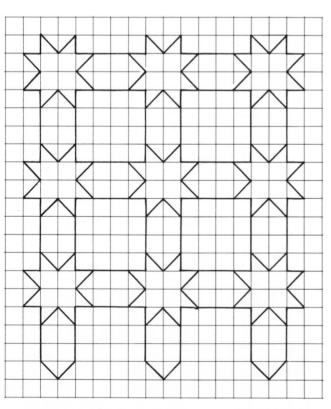

Pieced/Sawtooth Stars, Continued

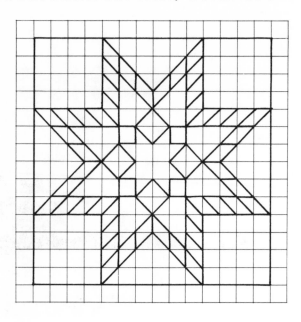

Variable/Ohio Stars

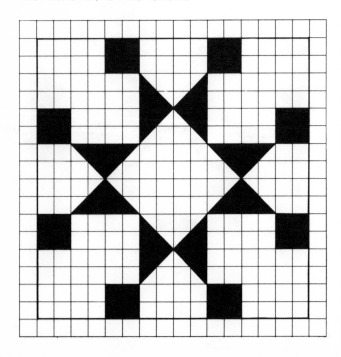
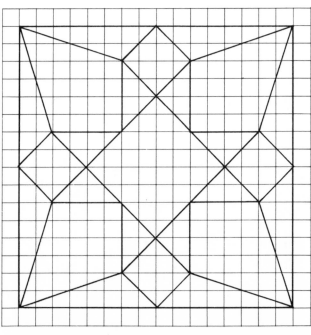

Variable/Ohio Stars, Continued

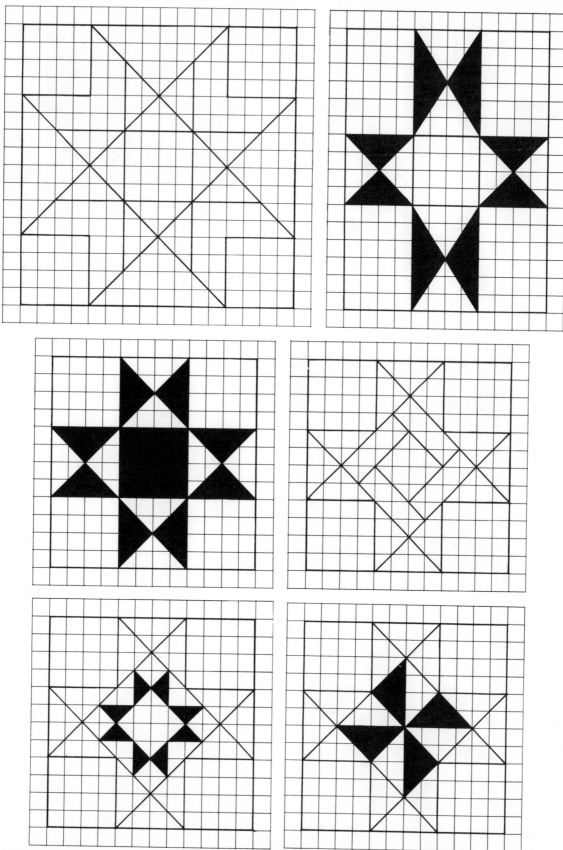

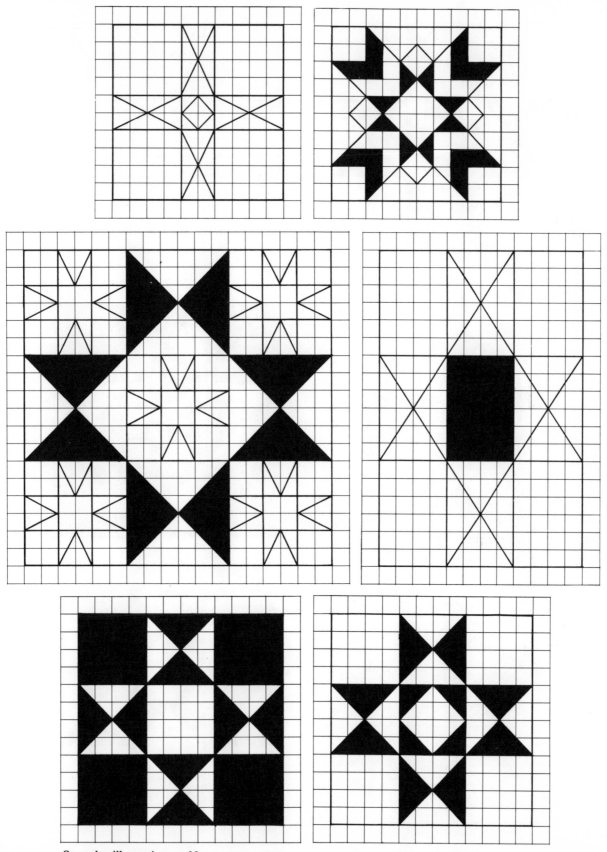

See color illustration, p. 38.

Variable/Ohio Stars, Continued

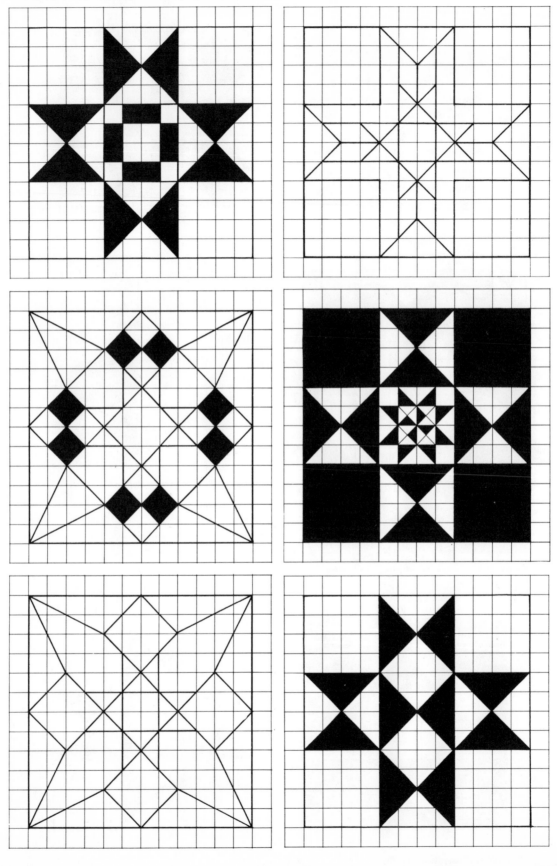

Variable/Ohio Stars, Continued

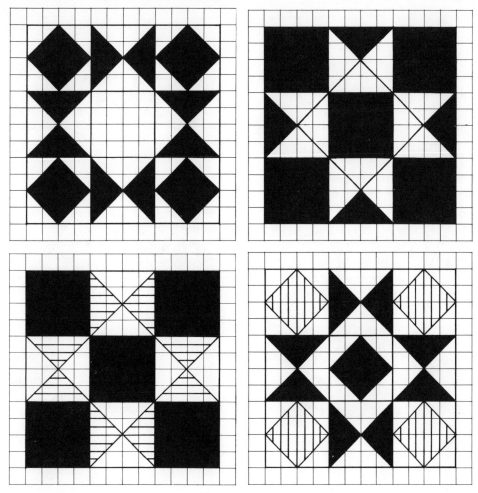

Regular Stars

6 x 6

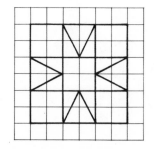 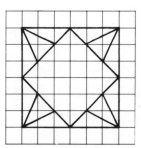  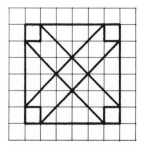

Regular Stars, Continued

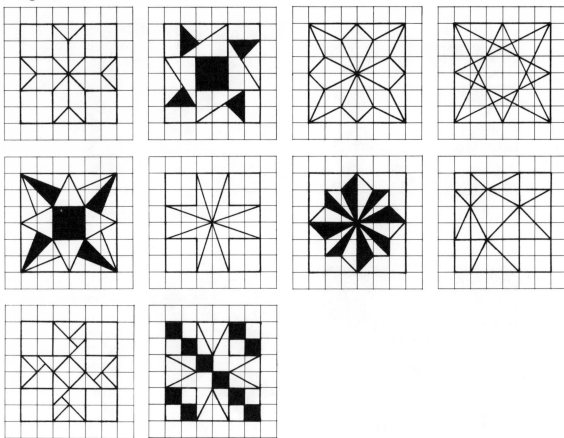

7 x 7

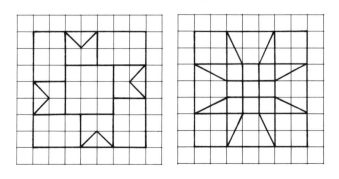

8 x 8

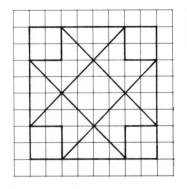

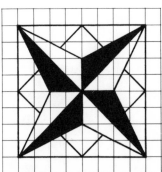

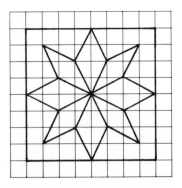

Regular Stars, Continued

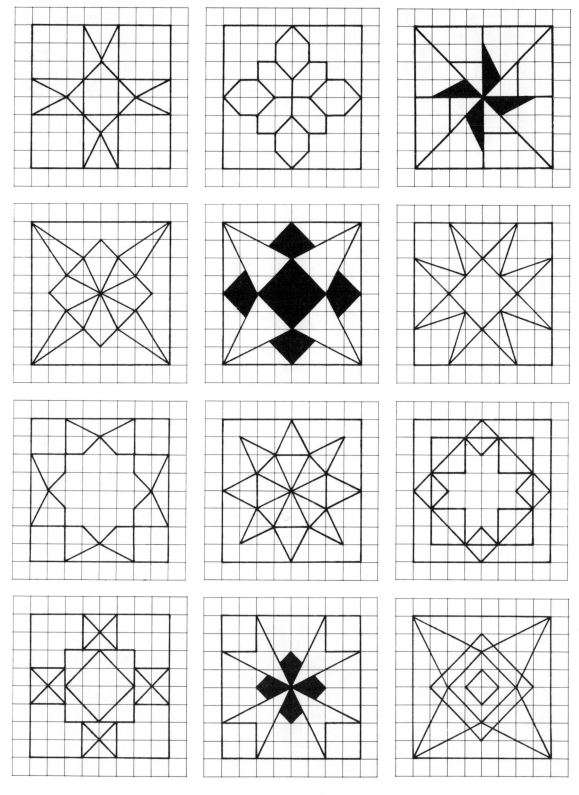

Regular Stars, Continued

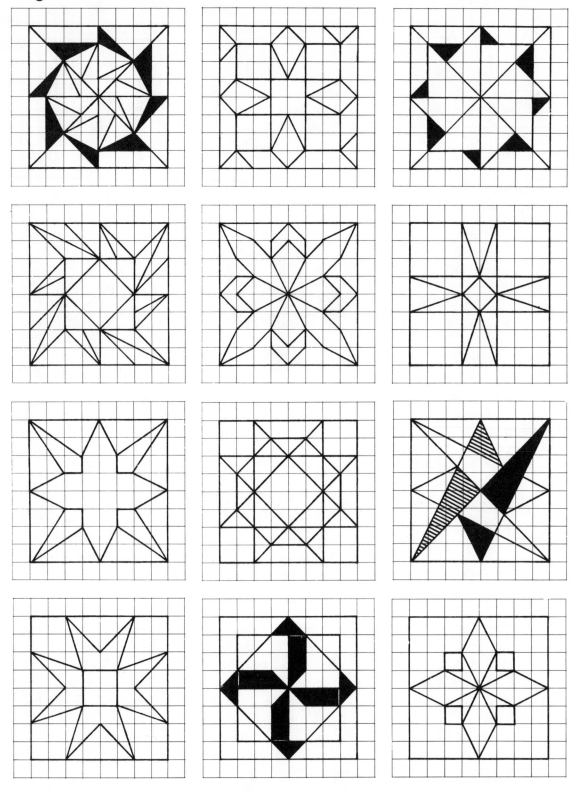

Regular Stars, Continued

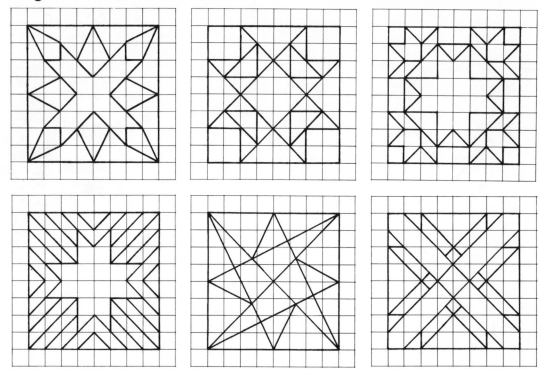

9 x 9

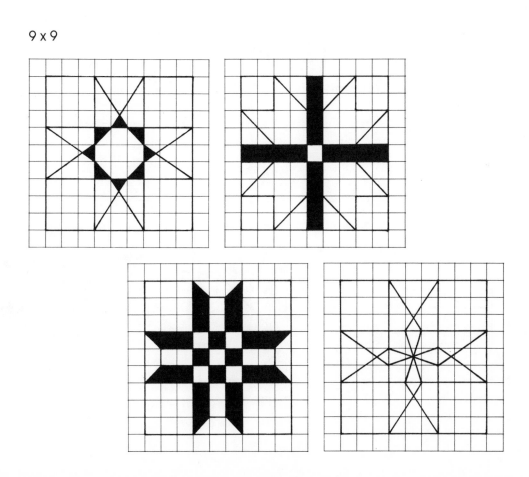

Regular Stars, Continued

10 x 10

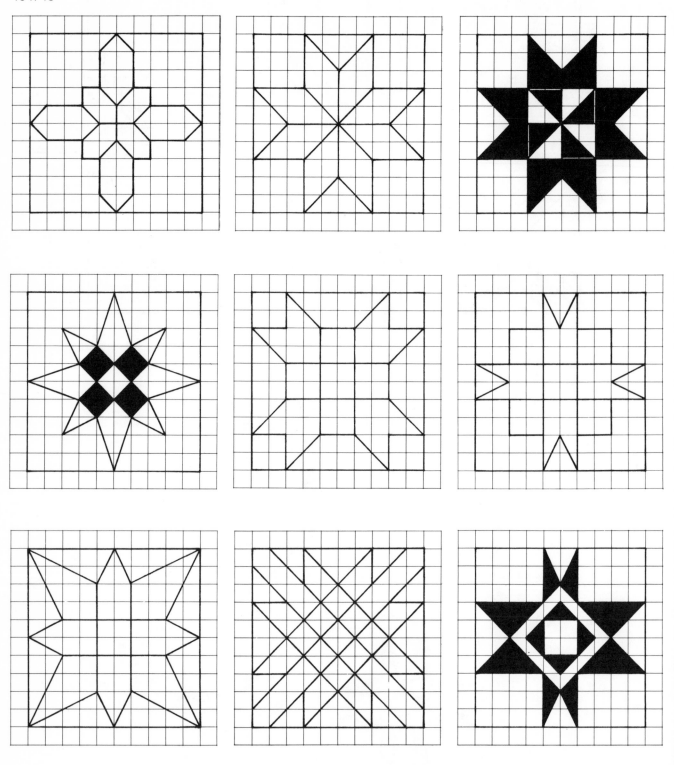

Regular Stars, Continued

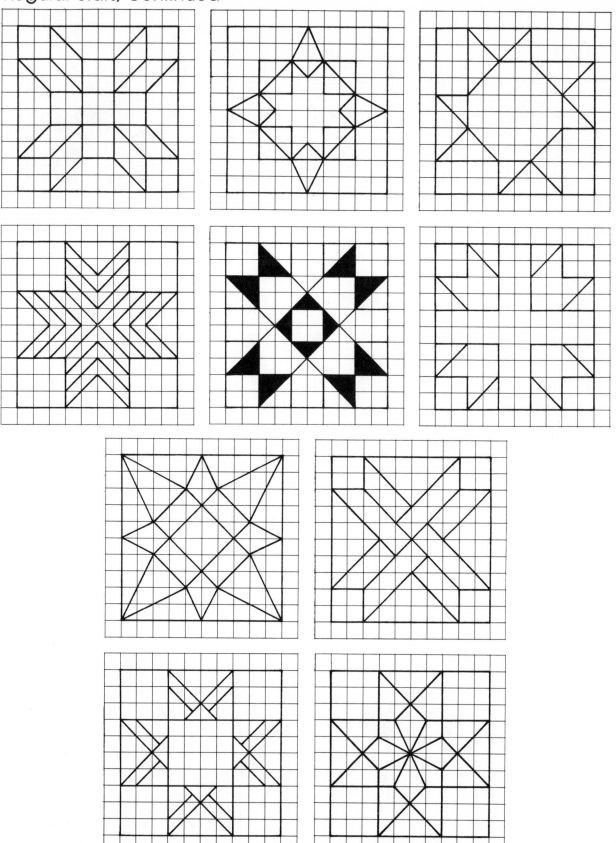

Regular Stars, Continued

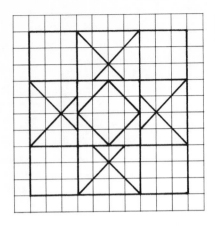
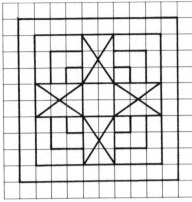
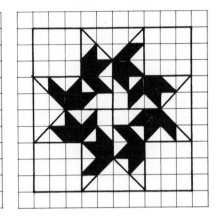

11 x 11

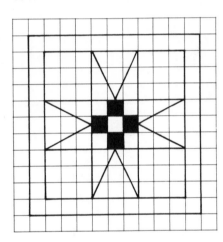
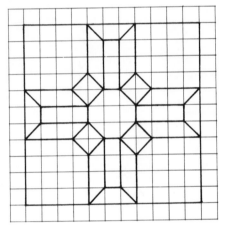

12 x 12

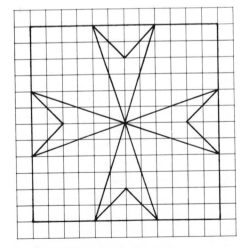
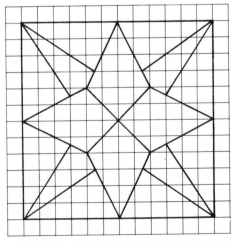

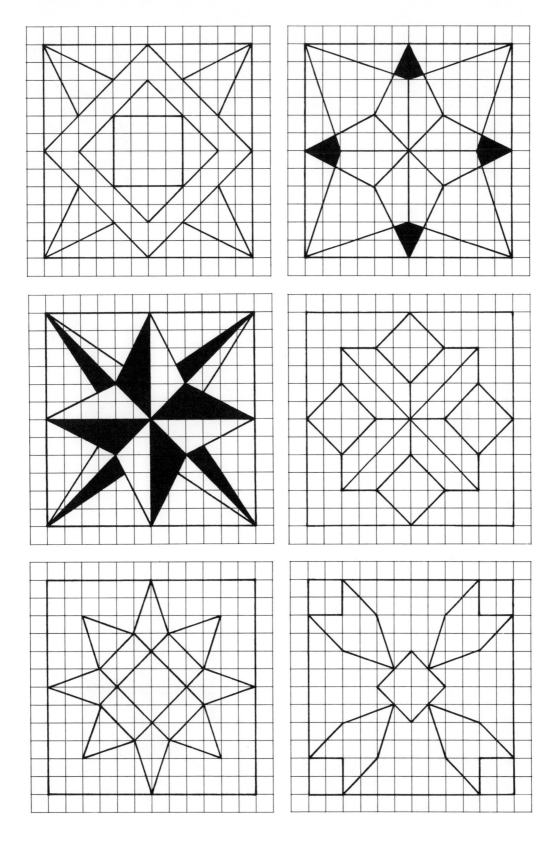

Regular Stars, Continued

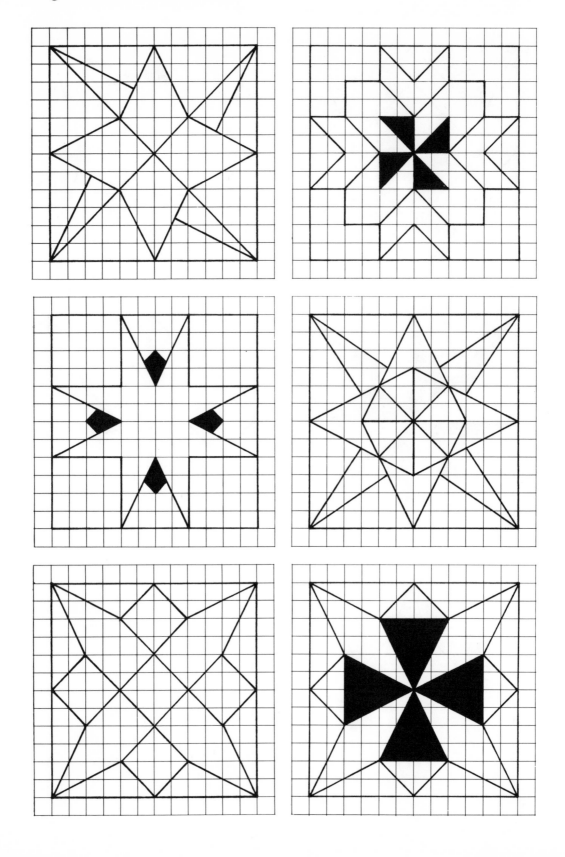

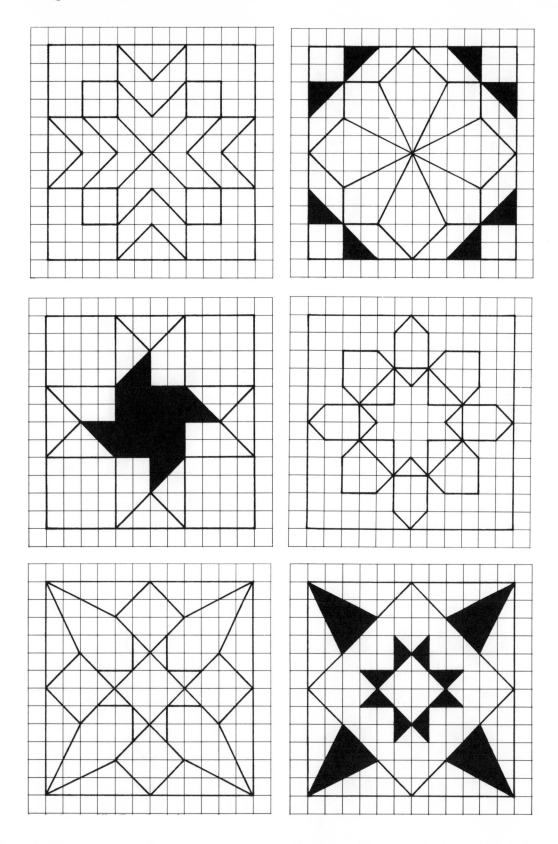

Regular Stars, Continued

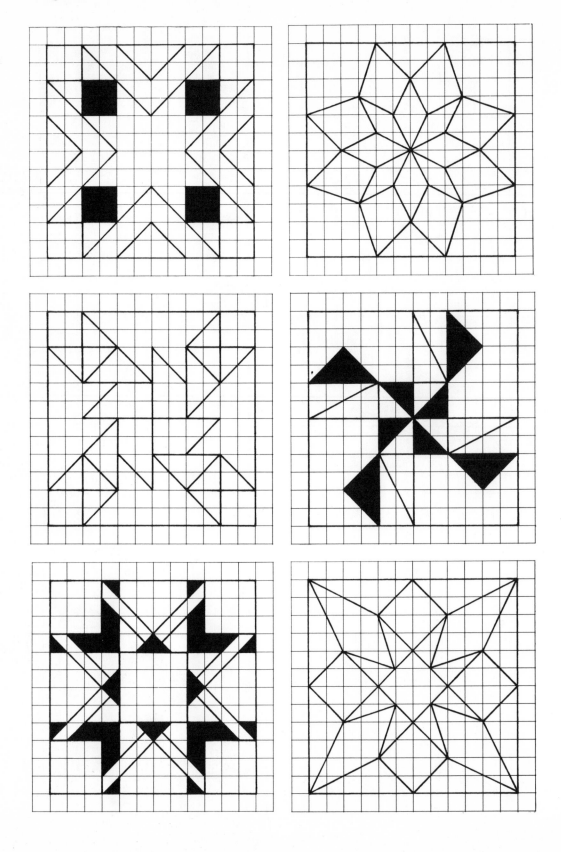

"Bursting Star," Stewart County, Tennessee, 1861-65, pieced cotton, 84″ x 82½″. See black-and-white design on p. 55. Photograph by David Luttrell, courtesy of Quilts of Tennessee. Collection of Emmett A. Roper, Jr.

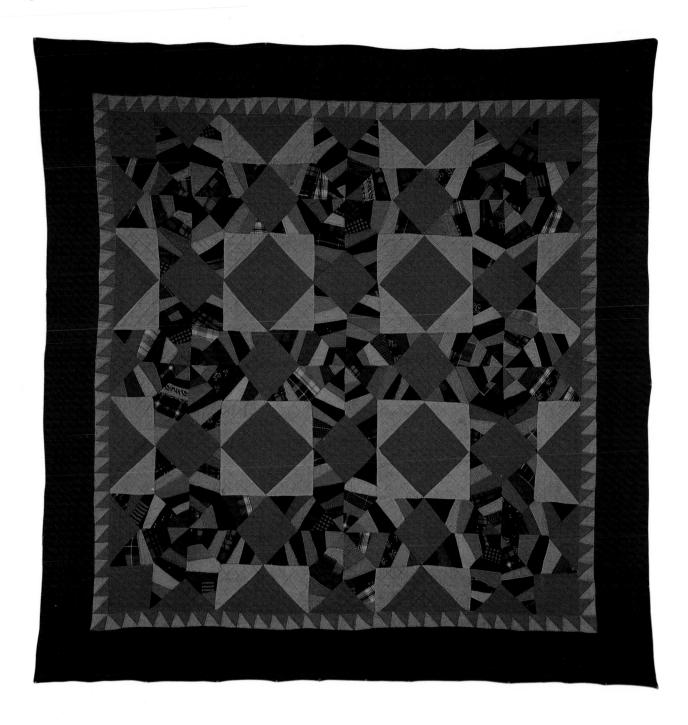

"String Star," Berks County, Pennsylvania, c. 1890, pieced wool, 80″ square. See black-and-white design on p. 102. Laura Fisher Antique Quilts and Americana.

"David and Goliath" variation, Ohio, c. 1910, pieced cotton 64″ x 79″. See black-and-white design of a star with more than eight points on p. 110. Collection of Phyllis Haders.

"Feathered Stars," Ohio, c. 1880, pieced cotton,
83″ x 87″. See black-and-white design of a
Feathered Star on p. 124. Collection of Phyllis
Haders.

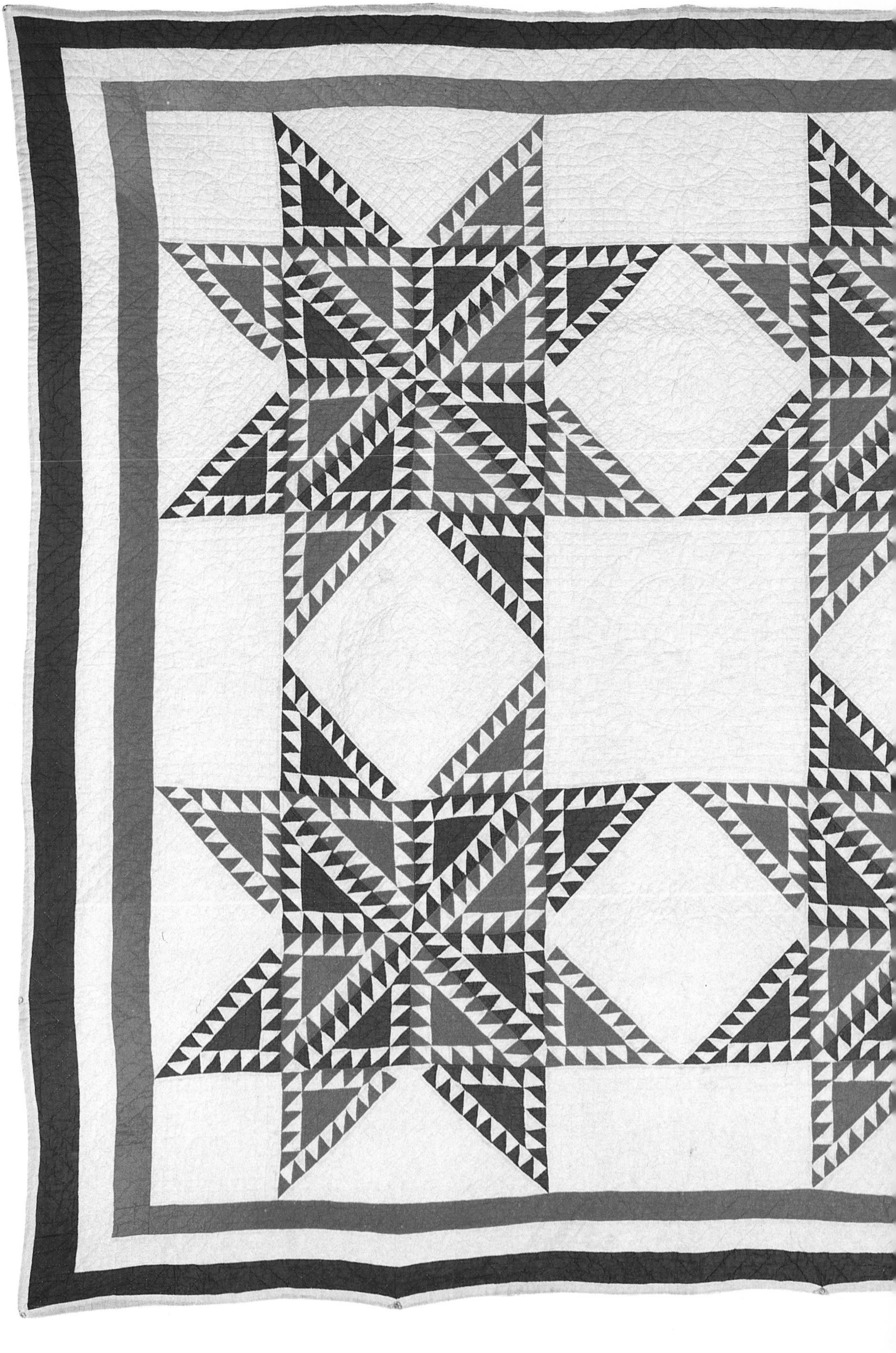

"Feathered Star," Midwest, c. 1920, pieced cotton,
74″ x 78″. See black-and-white design on p. 130.
Laura Fisher Antique Quilts and Americana.

"Kansas Baby," Kansas, c. 1861, pieced and appliquéd cotton, 36″ square. See black-and-white design on p. 136. Museum of American Folk Art, New York, N.Y. Gift of Phyllis Haders.

13 x 13

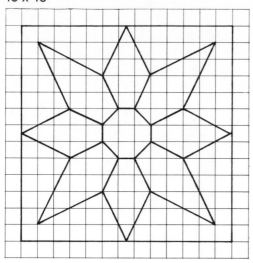

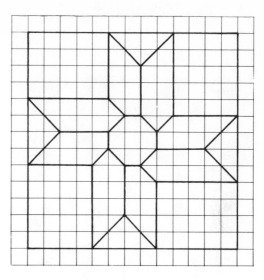

14 x 14

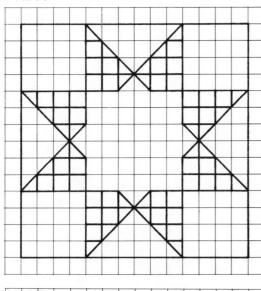

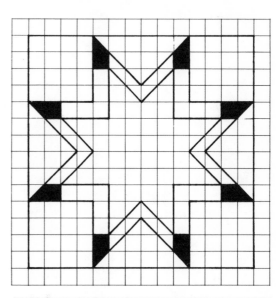

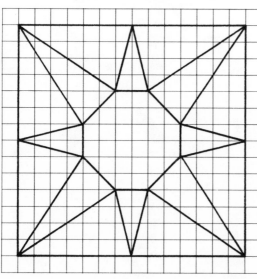

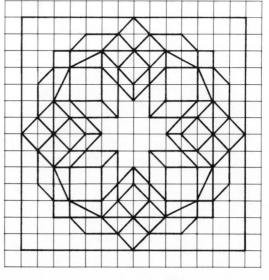

Regular Stars, Continued

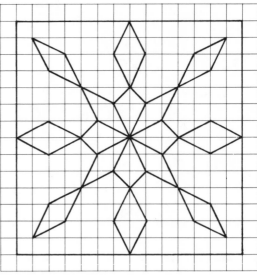

16 x 16

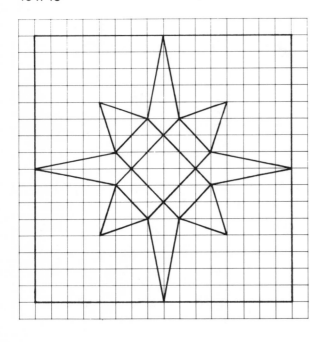

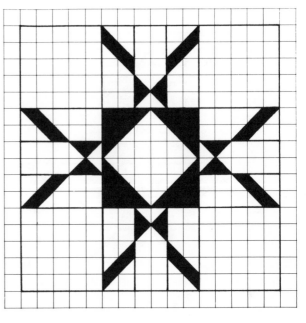

Regular Stars, Continued

18 x 18

20 x 20

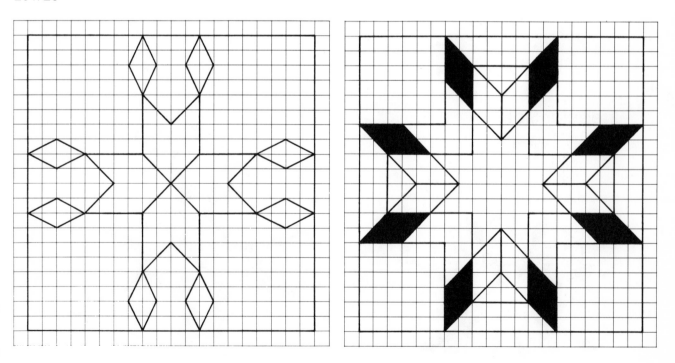

Regular Stars, Continued

22 x 22

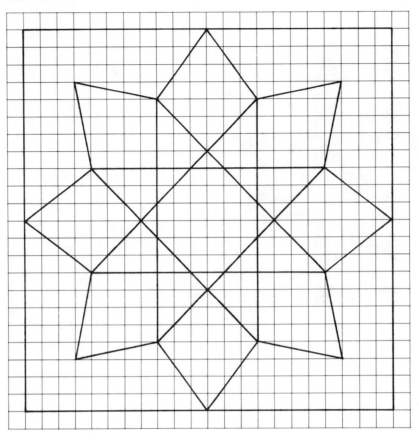

Irregular Stars

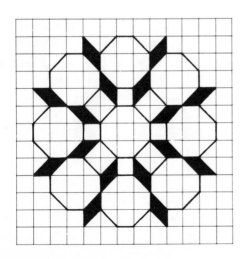

Irregular Stars, Continued

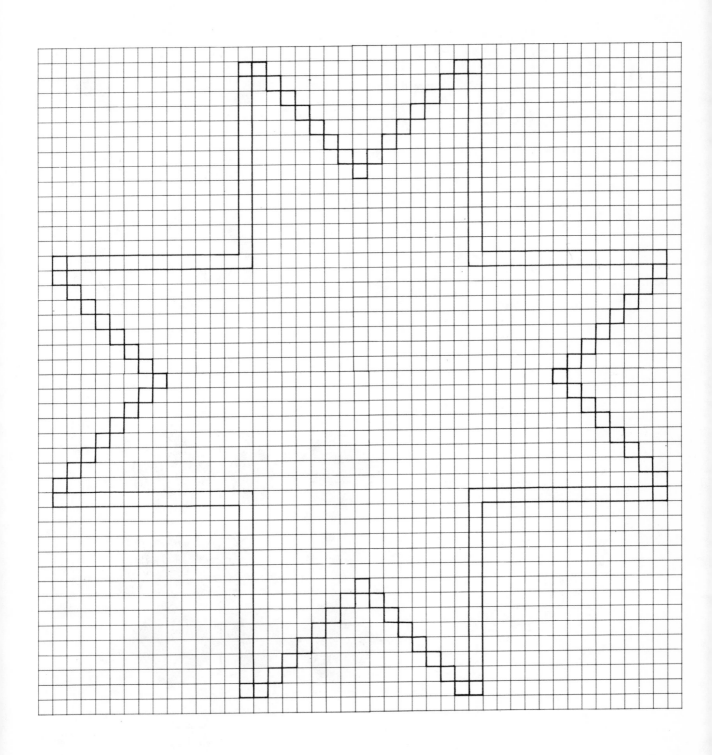

Irregular Stars, Continued

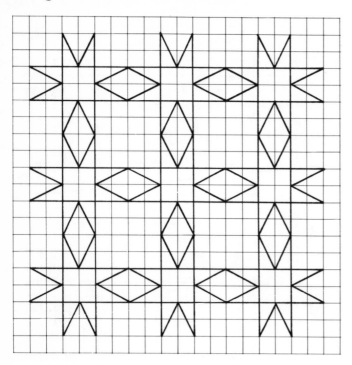

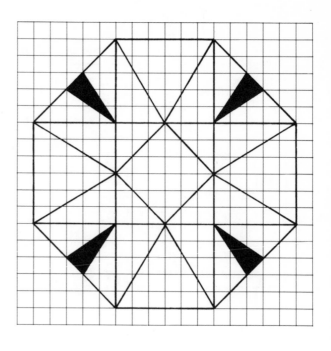

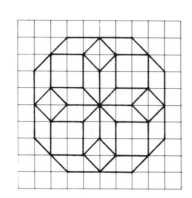

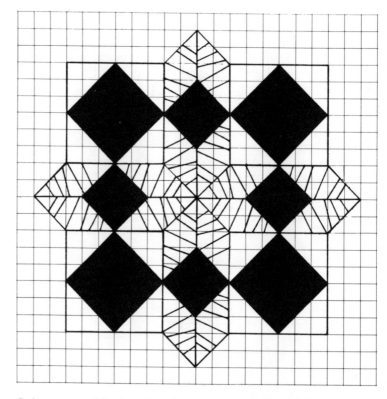

String star requiring irregular piecing.   See color illustration, p. 90.

Irregular Stars, Continued

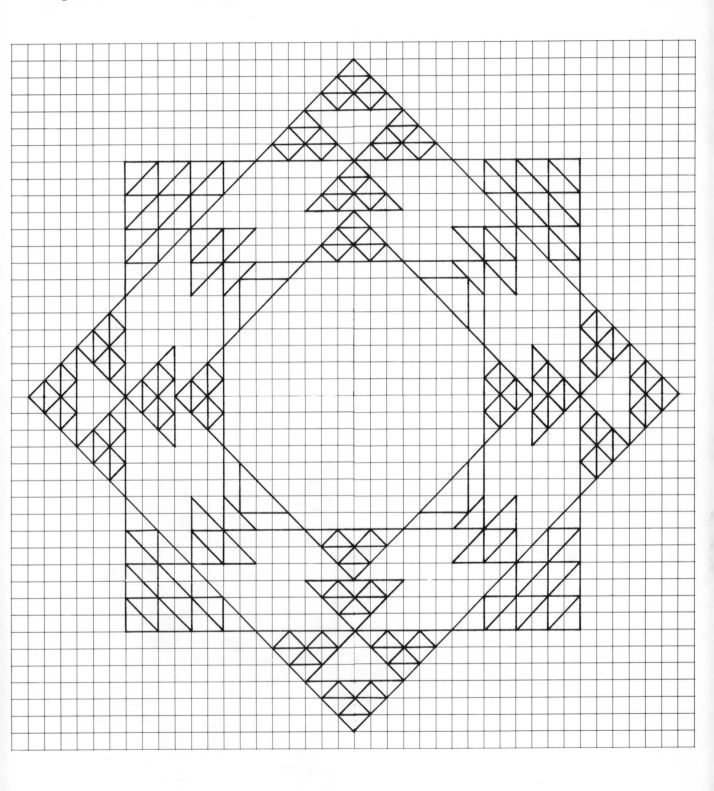

Irregular Stars, Continued

5. Stars of More than Eight Points

ALL of the stars in this chapter have more than eight points, mostly twelve and sixteen, though a few have as many as twenty-four. They are distinguished from sunbursts and mariner's compasses, two related patterns, by the irregularity of their points. Suns and compasses have points that are all exactly equal. Stars have some variation in the shape of their points. This difference is slight enough that if the quilter wants to do the sun and stars, it is probably better to pick stars with fewer points to emphasize their difference from the sun. If, however, a glorious Milky Way is desired, then a quilt of stars with more than eight points is a wonderful way to accomplish this.

Most of the stars are regular, drawn in squares, and organized like the eight-pointers—by their relative scale, beginning with stars that fit into an 8 x 8 grid and going up from there. The remaining irregular stars are drawn in hexagons or diamonds.

Regular Stars, Continued

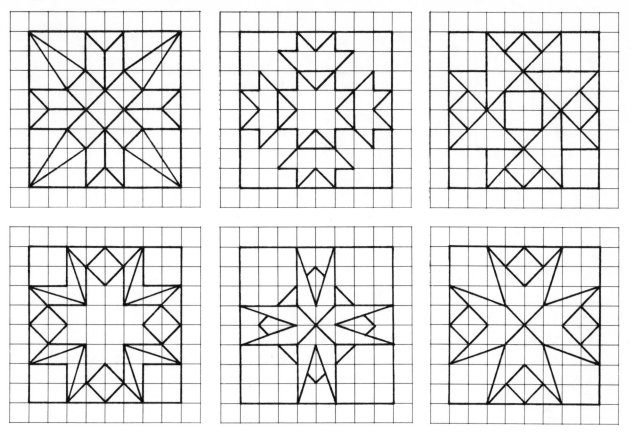

9 x 9

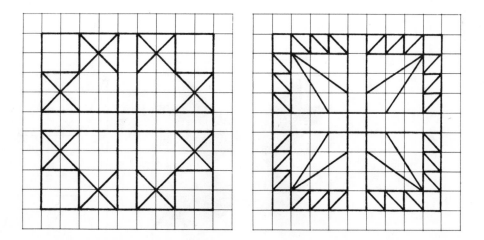

Regular Stars, Continued

10 x 10

12 x 12

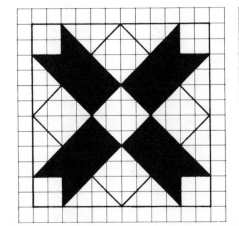
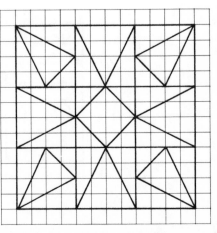

Regular Stars, Continued

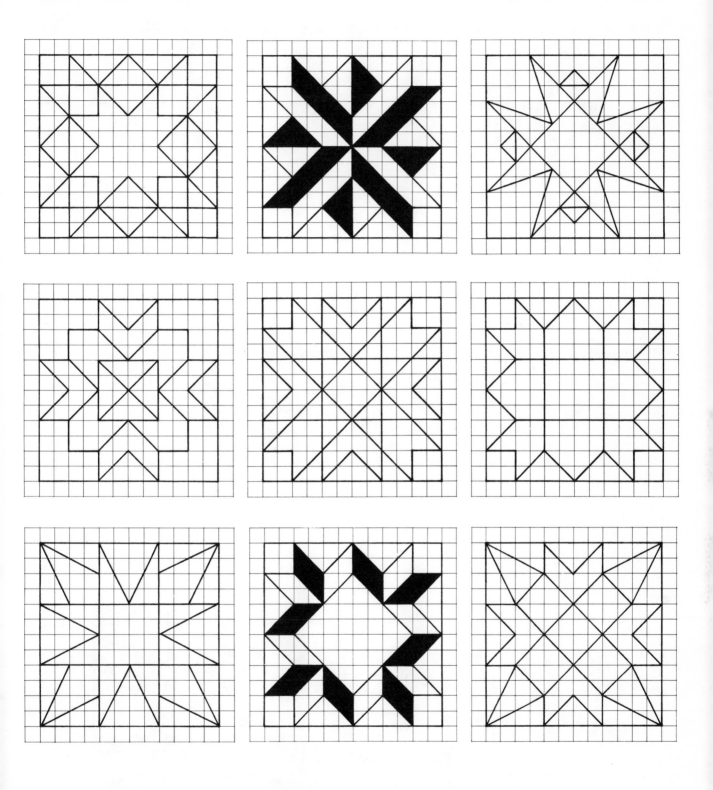

Regular Stars, Continued

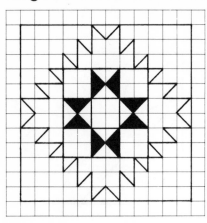

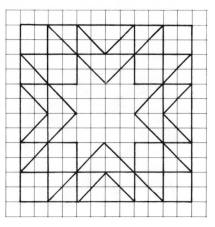

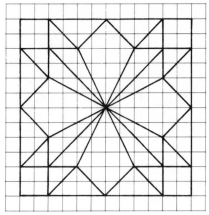

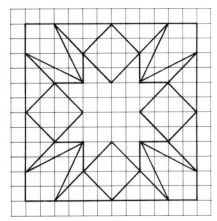

13 x 13

14 x 14

15 x 15

See color illustration, p. 91.

Regular Stars, Continued

16 x 16

Regular Stars, Continued

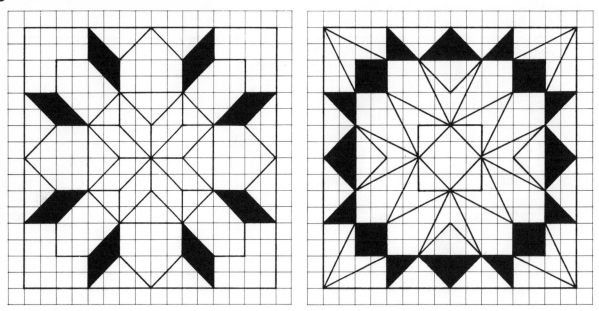

18 x 18

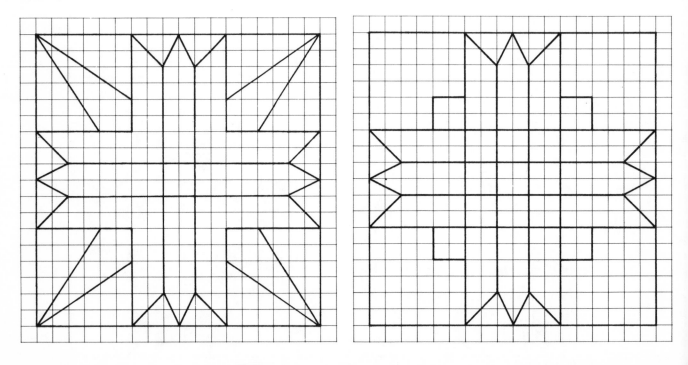

Regular Stars, Continued

20 x 20

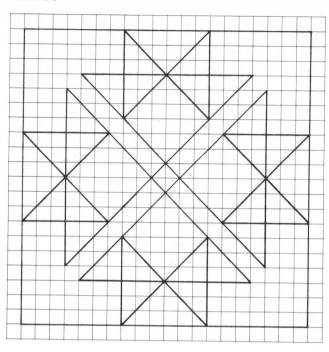

Irregular Stars

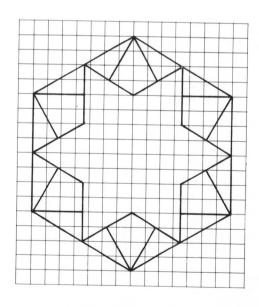

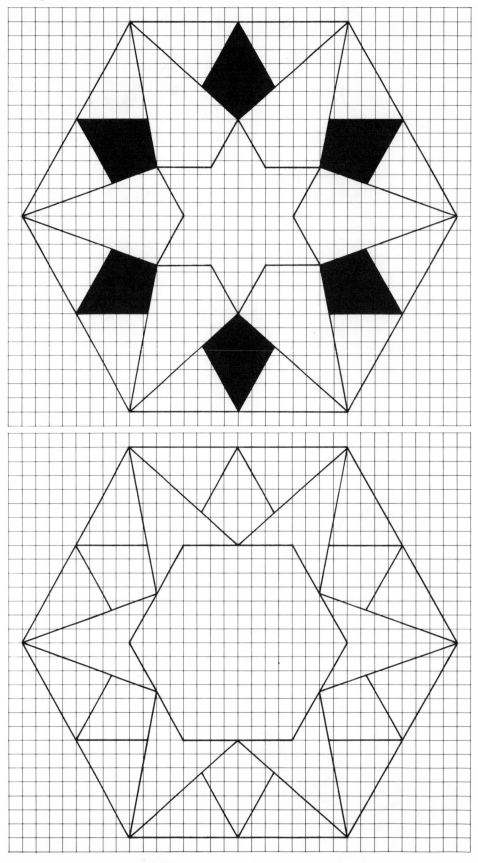

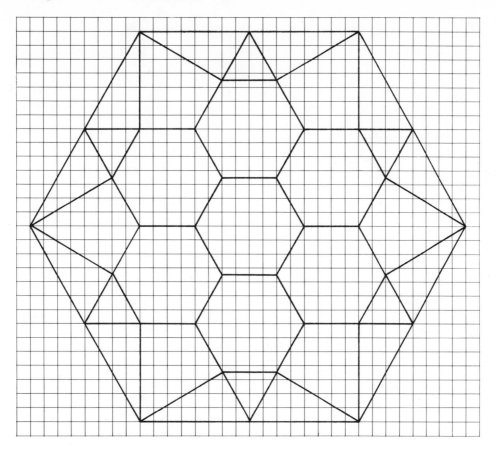

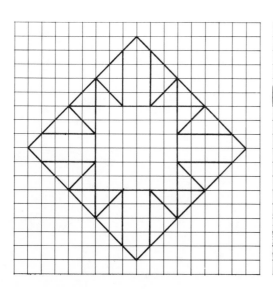

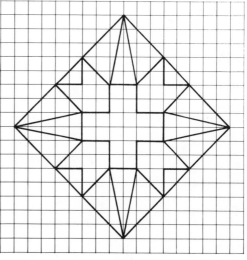

6. Feathered Stars

FEATHERED STARS are the movie queens and opera singers of the quilt world. They are usually larger than life, always glamorous, never easy. Feathered Stars are not started on a lark, to use up some scraps, or for a quick quilt. They demand planning, attention to detail, and pride in workmanship. Antique Feathered Stars are usually a single block, in two colors, with lavish quilting. Today, the Feathered Star is waiting to be rediscovered by quilters who want a challenge and a guaranteed eye-dazzler. The new quick quilting techniques will make the feathers go faster than they did in yesteryear. New color combinations and design ideas keep the Feathered Star a star among stars.

118

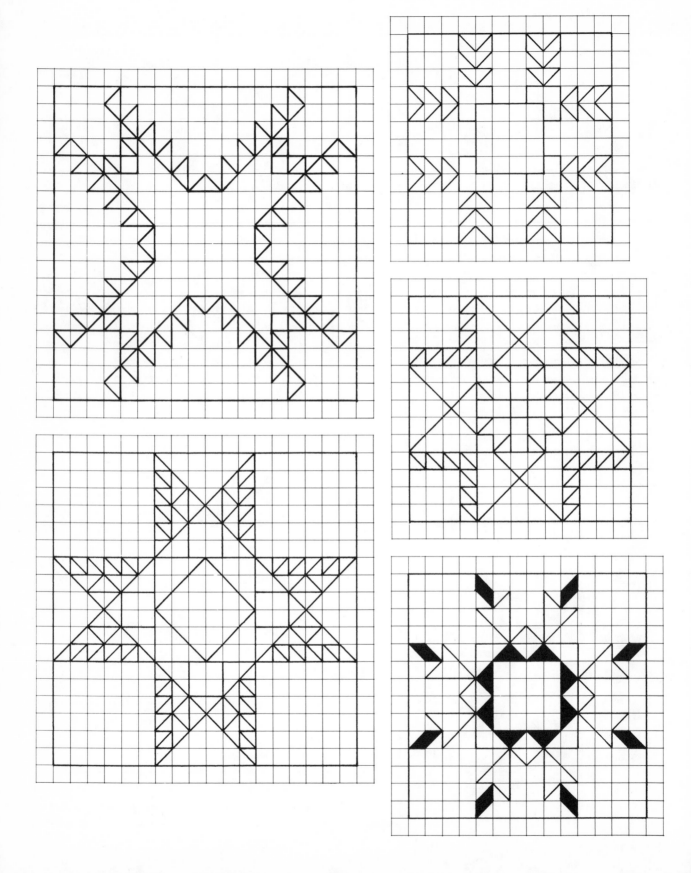

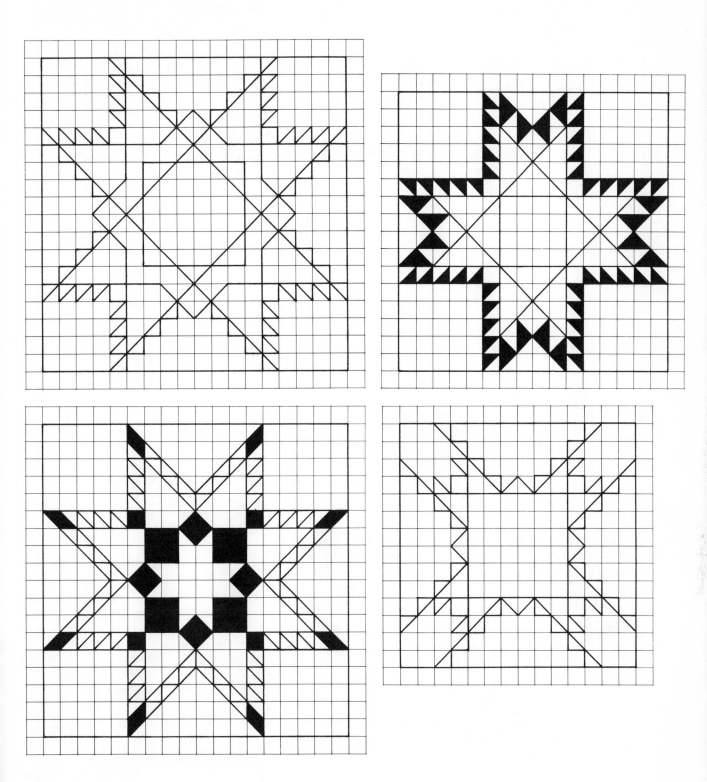

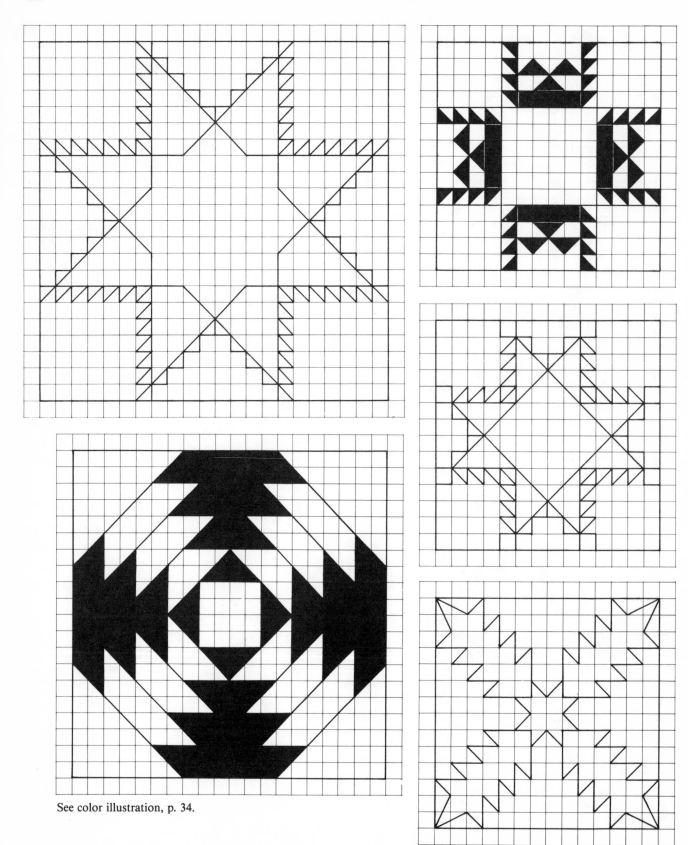

See color illustration, p. 34.

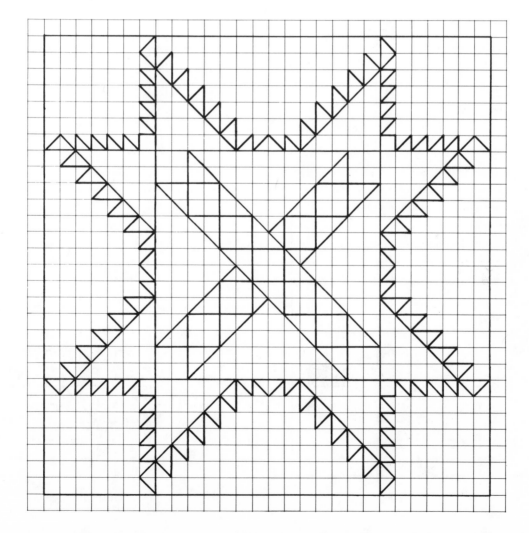

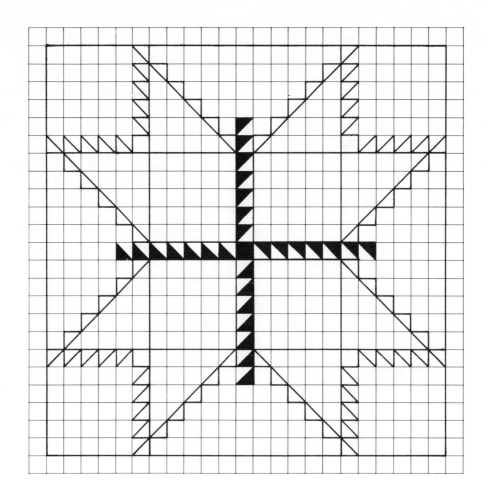

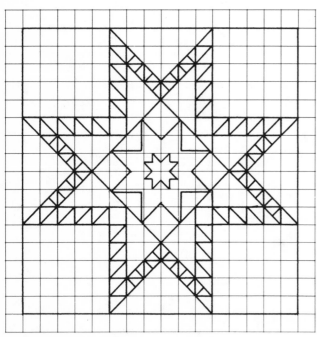

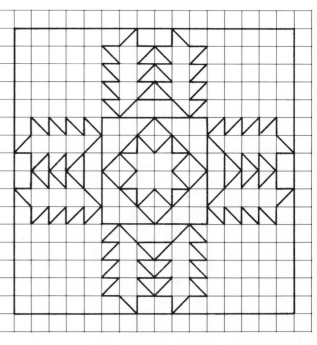

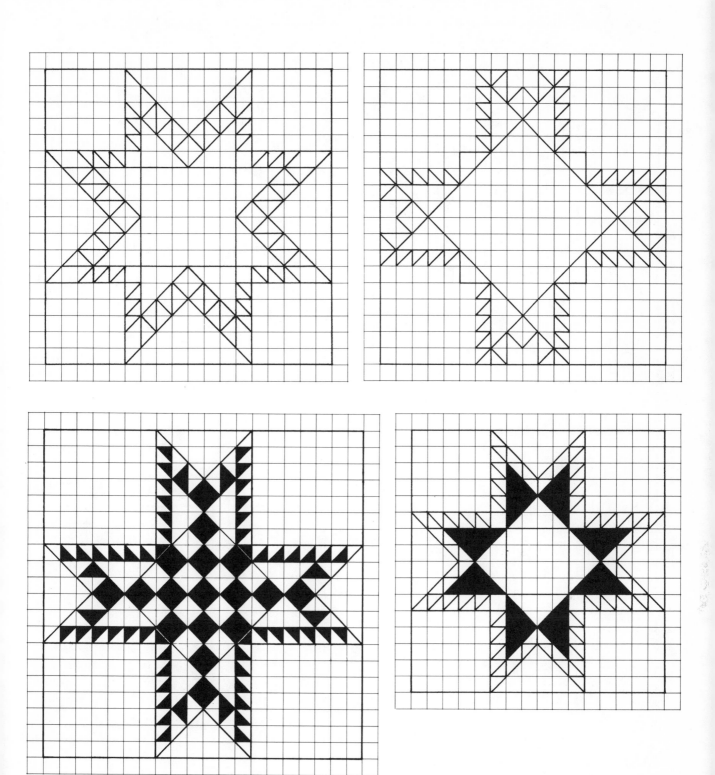

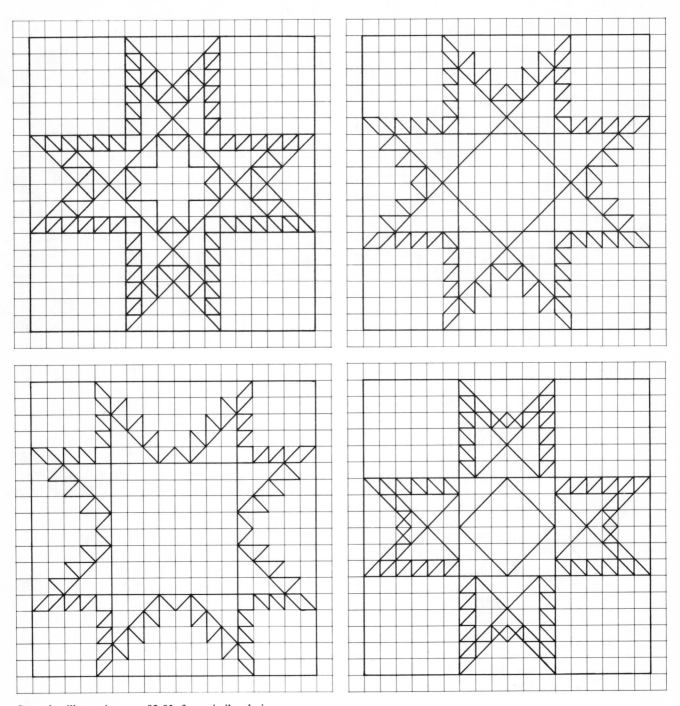

See color illustration, pp. 92-93, for a similar design.

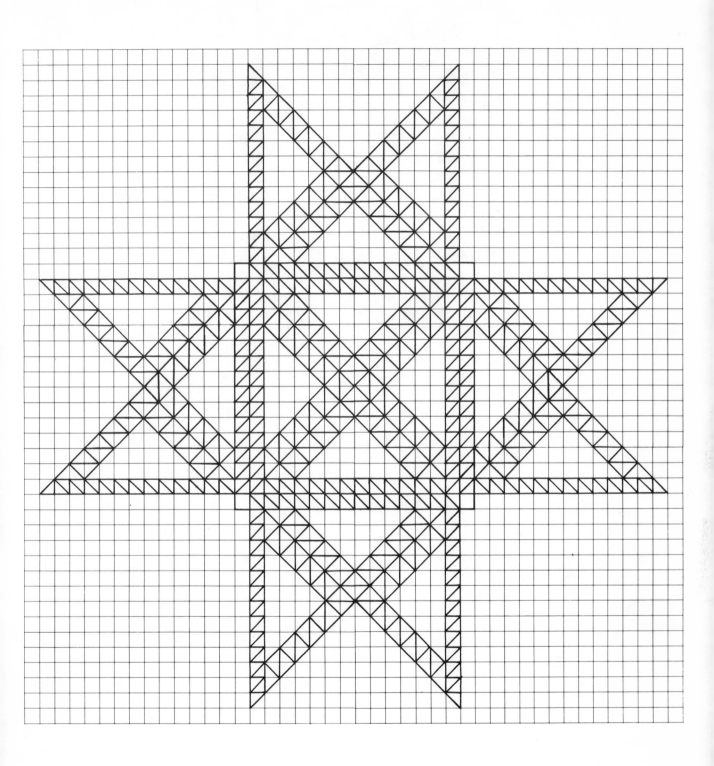

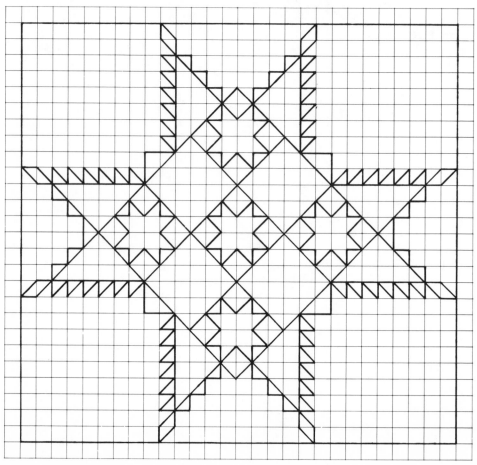

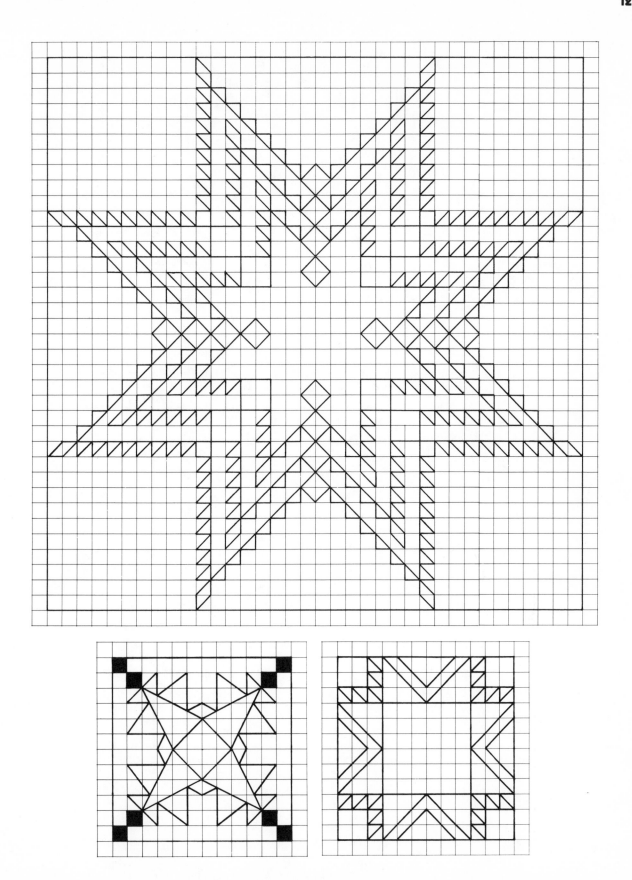

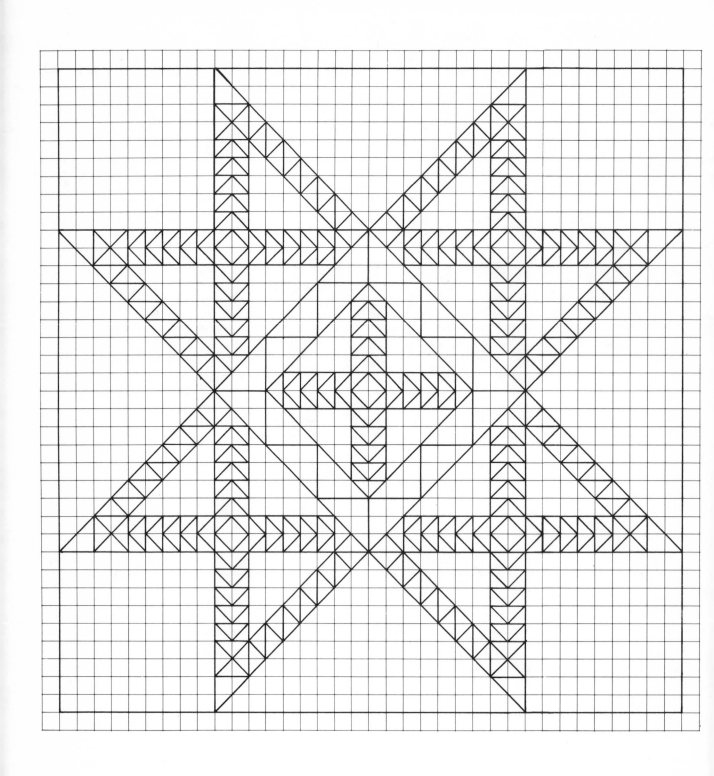

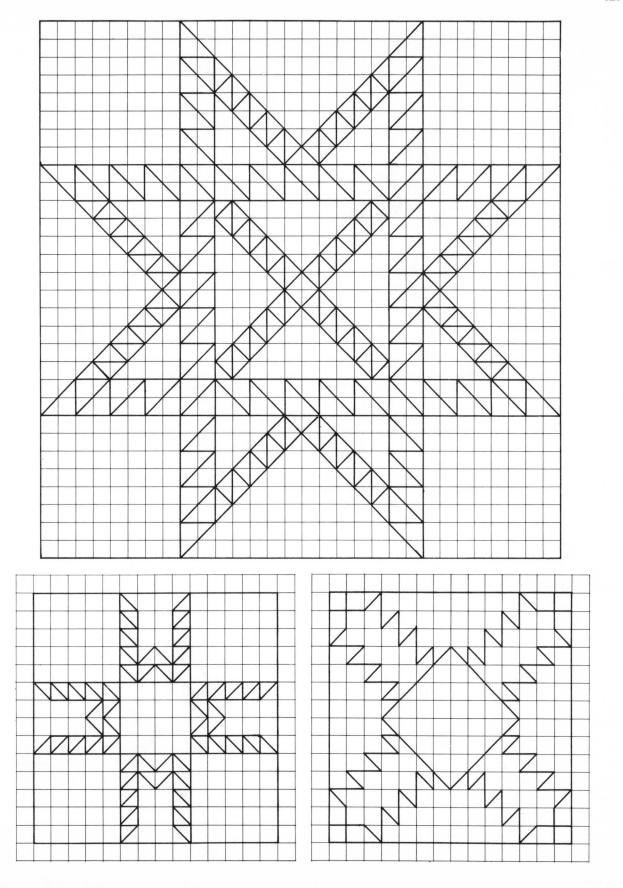

See color illustration, pp. 94-95.

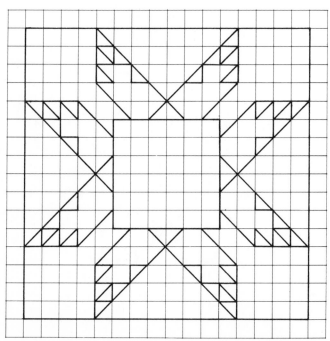

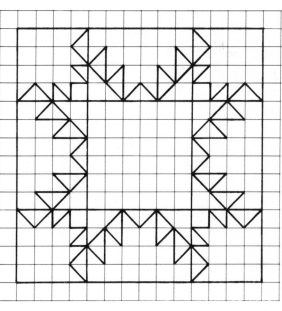

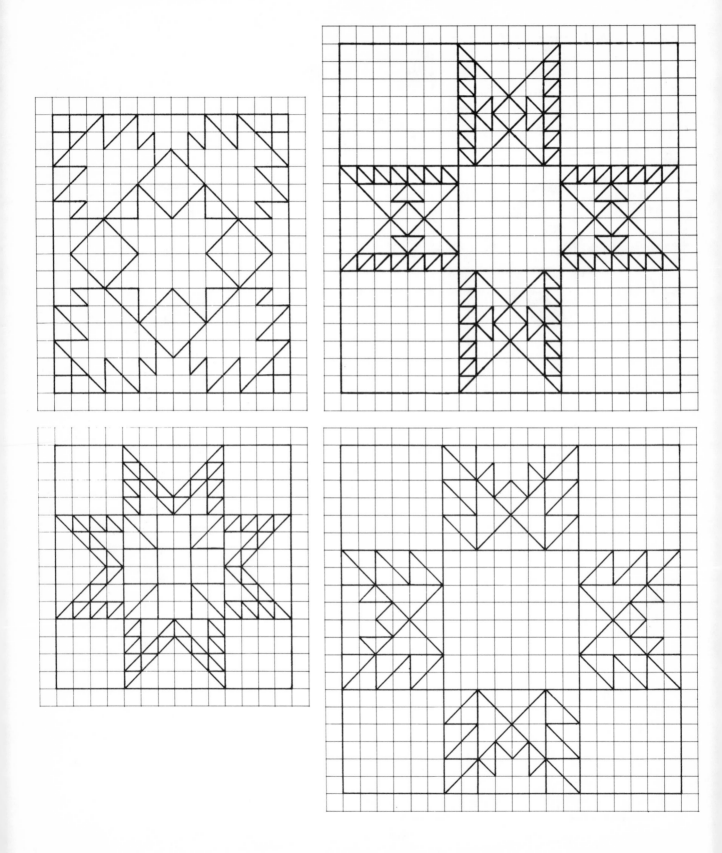

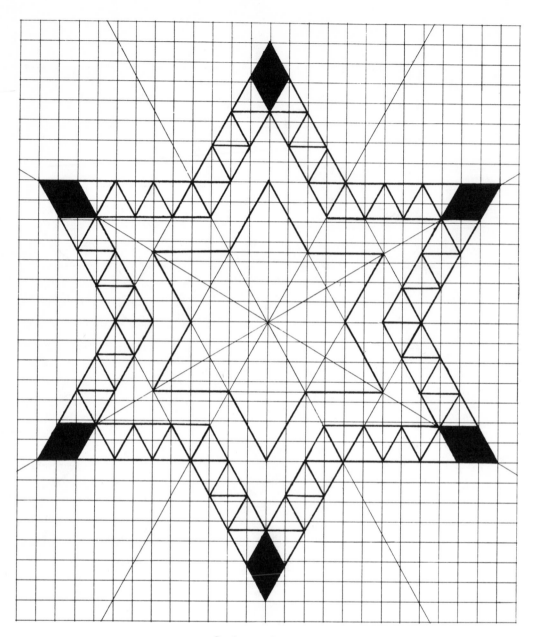

See instructions, p. 28.

7. Stars and Stripes and Shooting Stars

THIS chapter is a lagniappe . . . the New Orleans word for a baker's dozen, or a little something extra. The Stars and Stripes designs are like flags gone wrong. The components are there, but they aren't where they should be. If a proper flag is needed, try designing one with one of the simpler stars in this book. Or resort to my earlier book, *Patchwork Pictures,* where there are a number of flags to chose from.

The Shooting Stars designs all started out in their correct chapters for four, five, six, eight, or more pointed stars, but they demanded their freedom. They were insistent, some even saying they were really Halley's Comet and not ordinary stars at all. The author bowed to their greater wisdom and made a special place for them.

Stars and Stripes

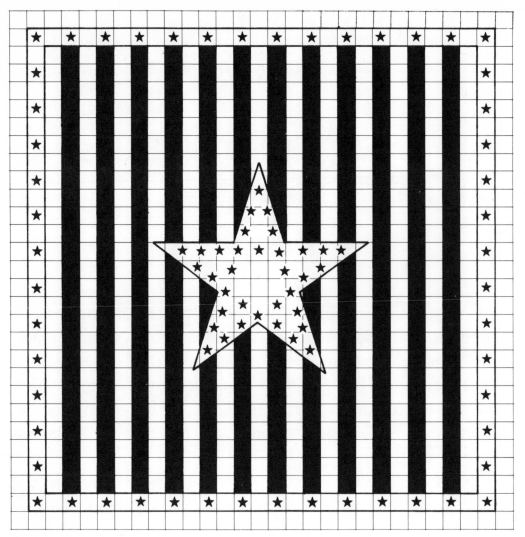

See color illustration, p. 96.

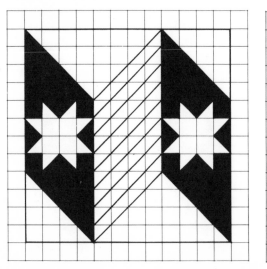

Stars and Stripes, Continued

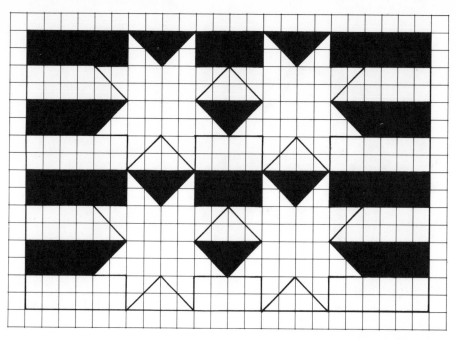

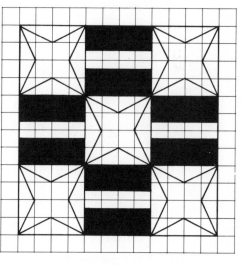

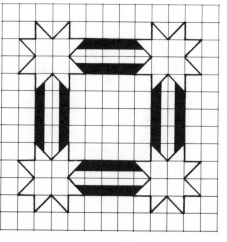

Shooting Stars

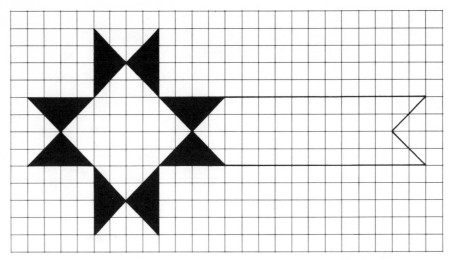

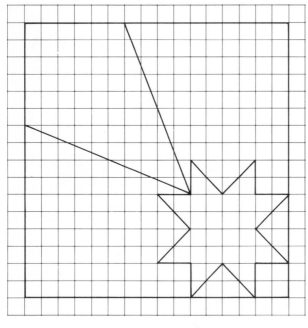

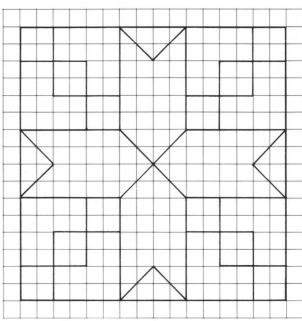

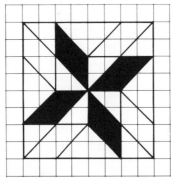

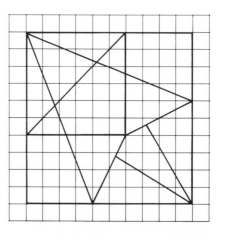

Shooting Stars, Continued

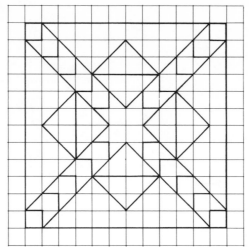

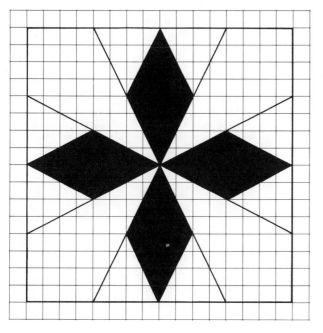

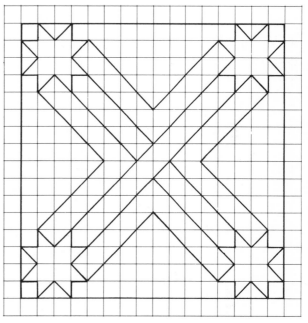

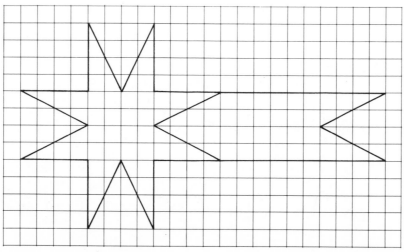

Shooting Stars, Continued

Shooting Stars, Continued

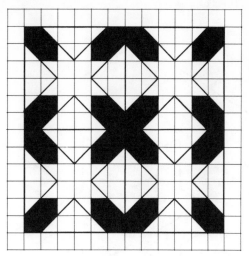

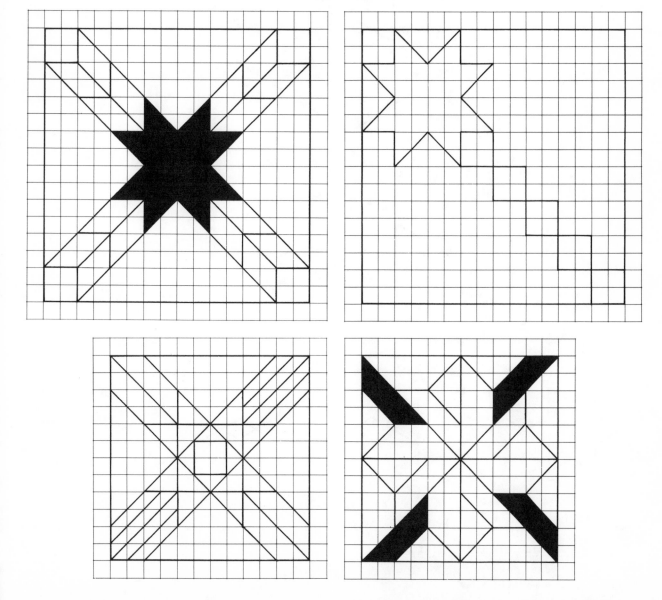

Shooting Stars, Continued

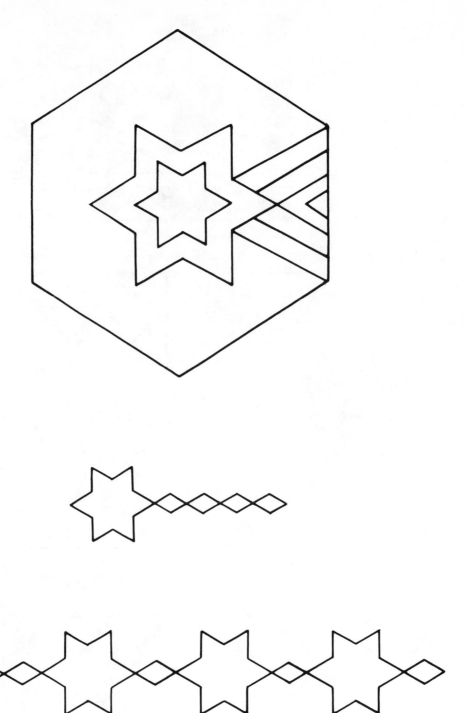

Shooting Stars, Continued

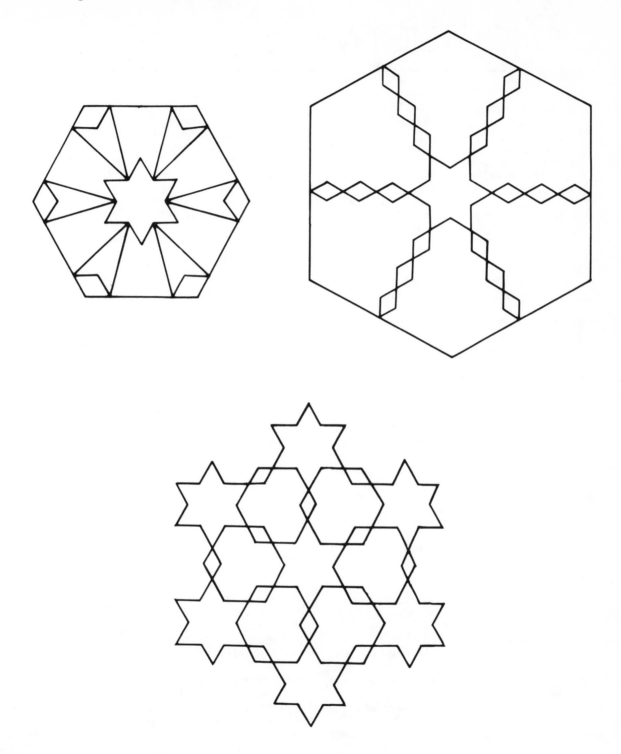

Bibliography

Albacete, M.J., Sharon D'Atri, and Jane Reeves. *Ohio Quilts: A Living Tradition.* Canton, Ohio: The Canton Art Institute, 1981.

Bannister, Barbara and Edna Paris Ford. *State Capitol Quilt Blocks.* New York: Dover Publications, Inc., 1977.

_____. *The United States Patchwork Pattern Book.* New York: Dover Publications, Inc., 1976.

Beyer, Jinny. *The Art and Technique of Creating Medallion Quilts.* McLean, Va.: EPM Publications, 1982.

_____. *Patchwork Patterns.* McLean, Va.: EPM Publications, 1979.

_____. *The Quilter's Album of Blocks and Borders.* McLean, Va.: EPM Publications, 1980.

Bishop, Robert. *The Knopf Collector's Guide to Antiques: Quilts, Coverlets, Rugs & Samplers.* New York: Alfred A. Knopf, 1982.

Brackman, Barbara. *An Encyclopedia of Pieced Quilt Patterns.* 8 vols. Lawrence, Kans.: 1982.

Carroll, Amy, ed. *The Pattern Library: Patchwork and Appliqué.* New York: Ballantine Books, 1981.

Dubois, Jean. *A Galaxy of Stars: America's Favorite Quilts.* Durango, Colo.: La Plata Press, 1976.

Finley, John and Jonathan Holstein. *Kentucky Quilts, 1800-1900.* Louisville, Ky.: The Kentucky Quilt Project, 1982.

Firelands Association for the Visual Arts. *Quilts and Carousels: Folk Art in the Firelands. A Sesquicentennial Exhibition.* Oberlin, Ohio: 1983.

Gutcheon, Beth. *The Perfect Patchwork Primer.* New York: David McKay Co., 1973.

Gutcheon, Jeffrey. *Diamond Patchwork.* New York: Alchemy Press, 1982.

Haders, Phyllis. *The Main Street Pocket Guide to Quilts.* Pittstown, N.J.: The Main Street Press, 1984.

_____. *Sunshine & Shadow: The Amish and Their Quilts.* Pittstown, N.J.: The Main Street Press, 1984.

Halgrimson, Jean. *Scraps Can Be Beautiful.* Edmonds, Wash.: 1979.

Hassel, Carla J. *Super Quilter II.* Des Moines, Ia.: Wallace-Homestead Book Co., 1982.

_____. *You Can Be A Super Quilter!* Lombard, Ill.: Wallace-Homestead Book Co., 1980.

Hinson, Delores A. *A Quilter's Companion.* New York: Arco Publishing Co., 1973.

_____. *A Second Quilter's Companion.* New York: Arco Publishing Co., 1981.

Holstein, Jonathan. *The Pieced Quilt, An American Design Tradition.* Greenwich, Ct.: New York Graphic Society, 1973.

Houck, Carter and Myron Miller. *American Quilts and How to Make Them.* New York: Charles Scribner's Sons, 1975.

Irwin, John Rice. *A People and Their Quilts.* Exton, Pa.: Schiffer Publishing Ltd., 1983.

Johannah, Barbara. *Continuous Curve Quilting.* Menlo Park, Calif.: Price of the Forest, 1980.

_____. *Quick Quilting.* New York: Drake Publishers, 1976.

Khin, Yvonne M. *The Collector's Dictionary of Quilt Names and Patterns.* Washington, D.C.: Acropolis Books, 1980.

LaBranche, Carol. *Patchwork Pictures: 1001 Patterns For Piecing.* Pittstown, N.J.: The Main Street Press, 1985.

McCloskey, Marsha. *The Feathered Star Sampler.* Bothell, Wash: That Patchwork Place, 1985.

McMorris, Penny. *Quilting: A Guide to Accompany the Television Series Produced by WBGU-TV.* Bowling Green, Ohio: Bowling Green University, 1982.

_____. *Quilting II: A Guide to Accompany the Television Series Produced by WBGU-TV.* Bowling Green, Ohio: Bowling Green University, 1982.

Malone, Maggie. *1001 Patchwork Designs.* New York: Sterling Publishing Co., 1982.

Martin, Judy. *Patchwork Book: Easy Lessons for Quilt Design and Construction.* New York: Charles Scribner's Sons, 1983.

Mills, Susan Winter. *Illustrated Index to Traditional American Quilts.* New York: Arco Publishing Co., 1980.

Nelson, Cyril I. and Carter Houck. *The Quilt Engagement Calendar Treasury.* New York: E.P. Dutton, 1982.

Olmsted, Janice. *A Dictionary of Patchwork Patterns.* Monrovia, Calif.: The Mail Pouch, 1976.

Orlofsky, Patsy and Myron. *Quilts in America.* New York: McGraw-Hill Book Co., 1974.

Pellman, Rachel and Kenneth. *Amish Crib Quilts.* Intercourse, Pa.: Good Books, 1985.

_____. *The World of Amish Quilts.* Intercourse, Pa.: Good Books, 1984.

The Quilt Digest. Vols. 1-3. San Francisco, Ca.: Kiracofe and Kile, 1983-85.

Robinson, Charlotte, ed. *The Artist and the Quilt.* New York: Alfred A. Knopf, 1983.

Safford, Carleton L. and Robert Bishop. *America's Quilts and Coverlets.* New York: E.P. Dutton & Co., 1972.

Helen Foresman Spencer Museum of Art. *Quilter's Choice: Quilts from the Museum Collection.* Lawrence, Kans.: 1978.

Tomlonson, Judy Shroeder. *Mennonite Quilts and Pieces.* Intercourse, Pa.: Good Books, 1985.

Vote, Marjean. *Patchwork Pleasure: A Pattern Identification Guide.* Des Moines, Ia.: Wallace-Homestead Book Co., 1960.

White, Margaret Evelyn, ed. *Quilts and Counterpanes in the Newark Museum.* Newark, N.J.: Newark Museum, 1948.

Wiss, Audrey and Douglas. *Folk Quilts and How to Recreate Them.* Pittstown, N.J.: The Main Street Press, 1983.

Wood, Kaye. *Quilt Like a Pro.* Greenville, Ohio: Extra Special Products, Inc., 1983.

Young, Blanche and Helen. *The Lone Star Quilt Handbook.* Oak View, Calif.: Young Publications, 1979.